ABOUT THE AUTHOR

Robert Nicholls has lived in the north-west since 1973, holding various professional positions in local government and other organisations. Born in 1952 in Sheffield, he was educated at High Storrs Grammar School, has a degree in Estate Management from Reading University and is qualified as a chartered surveyor. He recently gained an MBA from Lancaster University.

He is interested in local and transport history with particular emphasis on related economic development and land use changes. His previous publications include *Manchester's Narrow Gauge Railways* (1985), *Looking Back at Belle Vue* (1989), *Heyhead Church 1862–1992* (1992), *The Belle Vue Story* (1992), *Trafford Park, The First 100 Years* (1996), *Curiosities of Greater Manchester* (2004) and *Haveley Hey School – Seventy Years of Service to the Community* (2005). As well as contributing articles to magazines, he gives talks to local history societies.

CURIOSITIES OF
MERSEYSIDE

ROBERT NICHOLLS

SUTTON PUBLISHING

First published in 2005 by
Sutton Publishing Limited · Phoenix Mill
Thrupp · Stroud · Gloucestershire · GL5 2BU

British Library Cataloguing in Publication Data
A catalogue record for this book is available from the British Library.

ISBN 0-7509-3984-2

To those who lost their lives
at Hillsborough

Typeset in 10/11.5 pt Janson Text.
Typesetting and origination by
Sutton Publishing Limited.
Printed and bound in England by
J.H. Haynes & Co. Ltd, Sparkford.

CONTENTS

Visiting the Curiosities		6
Acknowledgements		6
Introduction		7
Map		8
1.	Liverpool	9
2.	Knowsley	73
3.	Sefton	81
4.	St Helens	103
5.	Wirral	123
	Index	174

VISITING THE CURIOSITIES

Most of the curiosities listed in this book are not tourist attractions in their own right, but can been seen, externally at least, without paying an admission fee. Many are visible from the road or from other freely accessible areas. A few have interiors where access might require payment of an admission charge. Where access is not possible, this is made quite clear in the 'Access' details given in the text. The curiosities can be visited either singly, or in groups by area. Those in central Liverpool are best visited on foot; others make ideal car outings. Most can be visited by public transport, and many can be seen by the less mobile.

ACKNOWLEDGEMENTS

Books of this nature can only be written with the willing assistance of a great many people. Much information has been garnered from visits to the local history libraries at Liverpool, Huyton, Crosby, Southport, St Helens, Birkenhead, Wallasey, Bebbington and Heswall. Valuable help has been given also by the archivists at Chester, Crosby (Mark Sargent), Knowsley (Rob O'Brien) and Wirral (Francesca Anyon). Books, guidebooks, the internet, tourist and publicity material have also been useful sources of information. Proper acknowledgement also needs to be given to all the local history authors whose painstaking research over the years makes a valuable contribution to this collection of curiosities.

Innumerable land and property owners need to be thanked for giving me permission to take photographs for this book. The staff and clergy at the various churches deserve particular thanks in this regard. Special thanks are also due to Mark Blundell, the Revd Roger Clarke, Alan Ford, John and Sue Gillin, Emlyn Jones, Gwyn Jones, Chris Makepeace, Linda and Gerry Miller, Alan Nixon, Ruth Scholefield, Steve Siddorn, the Revd Colin Smith and Rod Tann.

Organisations whose help is appreciated include Liverpool City Council Parks and Environment Service (Derek Dottie and Derrick Jones), Sefton Borough Council (Mark Wilde and Declan Kearney), Billinge Local History Society (Joe Taylor), the National Trust (Fountains Estate), the Joseph Williamson Society, St Mary's Church, Little Crosby (Paul Breen) and the Crosby Hall Educational Trust (Geoff Prest).

Picture credits are acknowledged to Liverpool Record Office at Liverpool Library (photo on page 31), Birkenhead Central Library (photo on page 145), Knowsley Library Service (photos on pages 77 lower and 80), Sefton Libraries (photos and illustrations on pages 39, 84 and 85), St Helens Libraries (photo on page 110) and Alan Godfrey map (extract on page 136).

INTRODUCTION

While researching this book I was often asked what was meant by the term 'curiosity'. It is a valid question, and one that is capable of somewhat different responses. In my case a curiosity is a building, structure, location or landform that is either rare or unusual architecturally, or is associated with a fascinating story, particularly one that might not have reached the pages of the history books.

Merseyside abounds with such things, and I have been faced with an embarrassment of riches. In the sister volume to this book, *Curiosities of Greater Manchester*, I gathered together details of over 140 sites; for this book the total is greater – and from a much smaller geographical area. Even then sites have had to be omitted or just referred to *en passant* for reasons of space.

Many of the area's curiosities are associated with the region's rich maritime past, when Liverpool was the second port of the Empire. Others are from more recent times, and include the area's contributions to the worlds of sport and popular music. Many reflect the time in which they were made and the personalities who created them. The curiosities in this book represent a microcosm of Merseyside's rich history, and each have a story to tell and a part to play in the historical development of the region.

The curiosities reflect and form part of their localities, contributing to the rich tapestry that gives the region its identity. The curiosities of Liverpool will be different to those of St Helens or Wirral, but their contributions to Merseyside are distinctive.

At the time of writing Liverpool is preparing to celebrate European Capital of Culture status in 2008. The curiosities in this book contain ample evidence of the justly deserved nature of that award. Liverpool and to an extent its adjoining districts are enjoying a renaissance with redevelopment and regeneration that will finally see an end to the problems of urban deprivation and dereliction that have blighted parts of Merseyside in recent decades.

Such processes involve change to the local environment. It is to be hoped that the contribution that Merseyside curiosities make to that environment will be appreciated and that care will be taken to protect that which is worth retaining.

The choice of curiosities that follows in these pages is inevitably a personal one. Readers will find many others.

1

CURIOSITIES OF LIVERPOOL

THE SYMBOL OF THE CITY

The Liver Birds, Royal Liver Building

Access

Located on top
of the Royal
Liver Building at
the Pier Head.

There really could never have been any doubt when it came to selecting the first and foremost curiosity of the City of Liverpool. The mythical Liver Bird, loosely based on the cormorant, is a potent and enduring symbol of the city. It is part of its coat of arms and currently used as an instantly recognisable logo for the local authority and one of the city's universities. It was even the name of a TV programme based in the city in the 1970s starring Nerys Hughes.

The Port of Liverpool was granted Letters Patent by King John in 1207 when he required a port to use for the conquest of Ireland. The town adopted a seal that incorporated the eagle of St John, the emblem of the Plantagenets, the royal house at the time. The seal was lost in 1644 when the town was sacked by the royalists in the Civil War.

In 1655 a second seal was ordered, but the local artist did not know how to draw an eagle, and the result is the cormorant-like creation, perhaps based on the cormorants that are common in the Mersey, and previously called 'laver birds', 'laver' (seaweed) being one of their foods. The birds are seen holding some in their beaks.

The two birds appeared in 1910 when the Royal Liver Building was constructed. Their addition to the building was an architectural masterstroke. They are 18ft tall, have wings 12ft long, are made of copper and take the overall height of the building to some 322ft above sea level. Aubrey Thomas, architect of the building, also designed the birds.

The female bird faces out to sea, while the male faces inland. Local folklore, as exemplified by the commentary on the river cruises, says that the female is awaiting her sailor's return (or alternatively looking to a future in new lands), while the male has a much more down-to-earth purpose and is looking to see if the pubs are open. The same commentary also says that they have never bred, but this is not true; the nearby Mersey Chambers adjoining St Nicholas's Church, has a smaller one, and another, formerly from the city's old St John's Market, is on display in the Museum of Liverpool Life.

The birds are reputed to bring good look to sailors. It is said that if ever these birds fly away then disaster will come to the city.

THE THREE GRACES

Royal Liver, Cunard and Mersey Docks Board Buildings, Pier Head

Access

To the north of the Albert Dock complex.

These three distinctive buildings make up a very impressive waterfront, recognisable to sailors the world over and regarded with great affection by residents of the city.

The southernmost building, the Mersey Docks and Harbour Board Building, was designed by Arthur Thornley and finished at a cost of £250,000 in 1907. The dome of the building is thought to have been taken from an alternative design submitted for the Anglican Cathedral in 1902.

The northernmost building is the Royal Liver Building, built for the insurance company of the same name between 1908 and 1911, and still the company's head office. Some say the design of the building was influenced by Chicago skyscrapers of the time. The clockfaces in the tower, below the Liver Birds, are 2ft wider than the clock in Westminster's Big Ben. It is sometimes claimed to be the largest clock in England. The building was reputedly the first concrete-framed multi-storey building in Britain. It was refurbished and cleaned in the 1980s and is open for free guided tours, which take place on weekday afternoons between April and September on a pre-booked basis. Part of the ground floor, which includes a magnificent courtyard complete with inlaid Spanish marble floor and replicas of the building's clockfaces, is open to the public during normal business hours.

The Cunard Building, designed by Willink & Thicknesse, was the last to be built, between 1914 and 1918. The Cunard Company has not been resident in the building for many years and it is now owned by Merseyside Pension Fund.

In recent years the proposal was put forward for a 'fourth grace' to be built on the site next to the Mersey Docks building. A futuristic design by Will Alsop was put forward, to be decorated with hieroglyphics depicting the city's 800-year history. Described as 'Liverpool's Guggenheim', the proposal, incorporating a round three-tier structure called the 'Cloud' would have incorporated offices, a hotel and community facilities. It was abandoned in early 2004 after spiralling costs made the scheme unviable. Another proposal is to build a new £10.5 million cruise liner terminal at the Pier Head.

An excellent way of seeing the Merseyside waterfront is on the River Explorer cruises that depart every hour from the Pier Head at weekends.
On the opposite side of the main road, at the corner of The Strand and James Street, are the old White Star Line offices, designed by Norman Shaw, and built in the same style as Scotland Yard in London, also designed by him.

A World War Altered the Purpose Behind this Memorial

Titanic *Engineers' Memorial, Pier Head*

Access

At the northern end of Canada Boulevard, next to St Nicholas Place.

This memorial, carved in white granite, was raised by public subscription to commemorate the men of the engine room in the *Titanic*. The onset of the First World War delayed its construction and it was decided that it would commemorate all marine engineers and engine room hands lost during the war.

Designed by Sir William Goscombe John, it was unveiled on 6 May 1916 without public ceremony. It cost £4,500, rather less than the £5,292 raised. The remainder was donated to the Liverpool Marine Engineers and Naval Architects Guild.

The memorial has gods on each corner representing the four elements: water, earth, air and fire. Sculpted panels show a greaser stripped to his waist, a stoker with shovel and other workers with crowbars and spanners.

There are many other memorials around the Pier Head, including the Cunard War Memorial, memorials to the Belgian and Netherlands merchant navies, a memorial listing all the local men who died in the Battle of the Atlantic, and one to the American troops who passed through the port during the Second World War.

A Memorial to a Liner Torpedoed in the First World War

Lusitania *Propeller, Albert Dock*

Access

Close to the
pedestrian bridge
that leads from
the Pier Head
into the Albert
Dock area.

The liner *Lusitania* was built for the Cunard company between 1905 and 1907 and was designed to counter the competition offered by newly built and fast German liners on the North Atlantic sea crossing. The Admiralty gave financial help in the form of loans. The *Lusitania* and its sister ship the *Mauretania* were described as the 'finest, fastest and largest steamers in the world' at the time. The *Lusitania* twice won the Blue Riband trophy for the fastest Atlantic crossing.

At the outbreak of the First World War the liner, as expected, was requisitioned by the Admiralty, but was soon returned to Cunard. It is thought that it often carried American-made munitions to England under the cover of its normal work as a passenger liner.

It was torpedoed by a German U-boat, *U20*, on 7 May 1915, on the final leg of its journey from New York, and sank in just 18 minutes near the Old Head of Kinsale in Ireland with the loss of over 1,200 lives. Although some 764 people were saved, over 100 Americans died, and the resulting tension between the (then neutral) United States of America and Germany started the long process that led to the USA joining the Allies in 1917.

The 23-ton bronze four-bladed propeller, with a cast steel cone, shown here was one of four on the ship fitted in 1909 that replaced the original three-bladed propellers. They rotated three times a second, and gave the ship an extra knot of speed, helping it to travel at over 26 knots (30mph). It was salvaged from the wreck with other items by a commercial firm in 1982, and it was bought by the Merseyside Maritime Museum in 1989. A cushion from the ship is also on display in the museum.

A memorial service for those who lost their lives in the tragedy is held at the propeller site every 7 May.

The Albert Dock is well worth a visit, with shopping, the Tate Gallery, Merseyside Maritime Museum and the Beatles Story display. It is a lasting tribute to Jesse Hartley, the Liverpool dock engineer, and forms the largest collection of Grade I listed buildings in Britain. It was opened in July 1846 by the Prince Consort. The whole complex was redeveloped between 1983 and 1988 and has been on the tourist trail ever since. The Dock Office, built in 1847 to the design of Philip Hardwick and now the home to Granada TV news, features a magnificent cast-iron colonnaded frontage.

THE SAILORS' CHURCH

Church of Our Lady and St Nicholas

This church is known as the Sailors' Church as it can be easily seen by ships docking in the nearby river, and because St Nicholas is the patron saint of sailors. The exact age of the original building is unknown, but it was certainly established as a Chapel of Ease in the fourteenth century. It is now the city's parish church.

When Liverpool was besieged in 1644 during the Civil War the church held prisoners of war for both sides at various times. The church also had strong links to the slave trade.

A disastrous event in its history occurred on Sunday 11 February 1810 when its spire fell in and killed some twenty-five people mainly young children under the age of fifteen from the Moorfields Charity. A new 120ft high tower, designed by Thomas Harris of Chester, was erected between 1811 and 1815 and was added to the main structure built in 1774. Further alterations were carried out during the nineteenth century, and a parish centre was added in the 1920s. The main body of the church was destroyed in the blitz, and was rebuilt between 1949 and 1952 to a design by Edward Butler, being re-dedicated on 18 October 1952.

The churchyard became one of Liverpool's public open spaces in the nineteenth century, and provides good views across the Mersey.

There are memorials to those who died in the Murmansk convoys of the Second World War, in the Liverpool and Bootle blitz of 1940 to 1942 and to the crew of the *Atlantic Conveyor*, which was lost in the Falklands War of the early 1980s.

A STONE TO MARK WHERE YOU COULD NOT BE ARRESTED

Sanctuary Stone, Castle Street

Access

In the carriageway of the road, about 100yds from the Town Hall.

This little curiosity is missed by thousands of Liverpudlians every day as they go about their business of getting to and from work. Although there is a small sign on a nearby building, the stone is now flush with the surface of Castle Street and is just a small circular area which is a different colour to the rest of the road surface.

It marked the limits of the fairs held in the city in the Middle Ages. If you had bought goods from a vendor and had not paid for them, you could still walk around the rest of the fair without being arrested for theft or debt, provided you stayed within the limits set by stones such as this. Once outside them, unless you had paid for your purchases, you would be arrested.

At the southern end of Castle Street, in Derby Square, is a huge memorial to Queen Victoria completed in 1905. It marks the site of Liverpool Castle, demolished in 1726.

A STATUE BROUGHT DOWN TO GROUND LEVEL

River Mersey, *Old Hall Street*

Access

Located on the south side of Old Hall Street, in front of the Cotton Exchange.

A heavily worn and weathered statue stands at pavement level outside what appears to be a modern office building. The statue was one of two which stood on the end towers of the former Liverpool Cotton Exchange, built between 1905 and 1906 to a design by Matear and Simion. The Cotton Exchange closed in the 1960s and the building's frontage was demolished and the interior re-modelled when the statue was placed in its current position. Two other statues, also from the old frontage and called *Navigation* and *Commerce*, stand in the courtyard of the building.

The statue is made of four blocks of Portland stone, mounted on an octagonal base. It comprises a heavily draped bearded male figure, clasping in his left hand an anchor, tiller and a length of rope. The right hand holds the lip of an urn from which liquid flows onto the head of a dolphin.

See also the full-sized carved bronze heads of tigers on the doors of the former bank at no. 7 in nearby Water Street. The building dates from 1850. In the past, visiting Lascar seamen (from India and the Far East) would rub the teeth of the tigers before walking to or from Paddy's Market (St Martin's Market, Scotland Road), to ensure good luck on their voyages.

MEMORIALS TO NELSON

Nelson Memorials, Exchange Flags and Springfield Park, Knotty Ash

Access

On Exchange Flags, immediately to the rear of the Town Hall. Springfield Park is located on the north side of East Prescot Road (A57).

Located behind the Town Hall is a circular monument, erected in 1813, and the city's first public sculpture. It was designed by Matthew Coles Wyatt and cast by Richard Westmacott to celebrate Horatio Nelson's victory at the Battle of Trafalgar.

It has been thought that the figures at the base of the statue are slaves, but in fact they are allegorical figures of Nelson's famous battles at Copenhagen, the Nile, Trafalgar and Cape St Vincent. The circular drum on which the monument sits was originally a ventilation shaft for an underground warehouse, now an underground car park.

The original monument intended for the site had been offered by a Mr Downward, a public-spirited sugar refiner, who had offered a stone shaft or 'needle'. When the designs of this modest memorial were shown to the city authorities they considered it too small, being described by one as only a 'half Nelson'. Mr Downward took his offering elsewhere, and erected it in the grounds of his own house, Springfield, at Knotty Ash, which is now a public park.

The Springfield Park monument is now showing signs of wear and vandalism. On it is a modern plaque with the words:

> Sacred to the memory of the illustrious NELSON who graciously fell in defence of his country and to whose skill and valour BRITONS are indebted for domestic security and tranquil enjoyment of the produce of their industry.

HEADQUARTERS OF THE BATTLE OF THE ATLANTIC

Western Approaches Museum

Access

On Rumford Street, between Tithebarn Street and Water Street. The museum is open daily except Fridays and Sundays.

The basement of the then relatively new Derby House is from where the Anglo-American air-sea campaign in the North Atlantic was controlled during the Second World War. It was taken over in February 1941 after it had been decided that the previous operations centre in Plymouth was too vulnerable to enemy attack. The decision to set up the new Command Centre was taken by Admiral Sir Percy Noble. It was one of a series of Combined Operations headquarters used by the Royal Navy and Royal Air Force.

Over 50,000 sq. ft of space was used, comprising over 100 rooms, the most important being the Operations Room, sometimes called 'the Citadel' or 'the Dungeon' by those who worked in it, where the day-to-day strategic decisions were taken.

In June 1942 additional rooms were taken on the top floor of the adjoining Exchange Building for the Western Approaches Tactical Unit where enemy tactics were studied in detail and training in counter measures was undertaken.

The museum tour only takes visitors around a small proportion of the original accommodation, but includes the main Operations Room, Admirals Room and teleprinter stations. Some wartime electronic equipment is on display and has been restored to use by enthusiasts. Other rooms have exhibitions on more general Second World War themes.

LIVERPOOL'S OLDEST PUBLIC HOUSE

Ye Hole in ye Wall, Hackins Hey

Access

On Hackins Hey,
which runs
between Dale
Street and
Tithebarn Street.

Dating from 1726, and located on one of the city's medieval streets, Ye Hole in ye Wall is believed to be Liverpool's oldest pub. The interior is more modern, either late Victorian or early twentieth century, with much wood panelling and leaded glass partitions. There are many small rooms in the pub. The telephone cubicle has a brass-studded door making it look like the door to a padded cell.

Thankfully, the pub has not 'moved with the times', and its clientele clearly appreciate this. One innovation, however, was to remove the men only restriction in 1976.

See also the Carnarvon Castle on Tarleton Street in the central shopping area. Dating from the late nineteenth century, this is the sole survivor of eight pubs once on this street. It stands out from its more modern neighbours by having a notable ceramic frontage. The interior is traditional with wood panelling in the rear room, and displays of old Dinky toys and beer glasses in the front room.

THE MOST FAMOUS CLUB IN THE WORLD

The Cavern Club, Mathew Street

Access

On the southern side of Mathew Street.

This is not quite the original Cavern Club, but a near replica. It has the same postal address (10 Mathew Street) and occupies half of the site.

The club first opened on 16 January 1957. It first featured skiffle groups, and in July 1957 there was an appearance by the Quarrymen, the forerunners to the Beatles. Between 21 February 1961 and 3 August 1963 the Beatles played at the club 275 times. Many of their early sessions were at lunchtime, attracting a whole new audience, including Brian Epstein, who became their manager in December 1961. The club's low ceiling and interlocking arches gave the place a special atmosphere.

The Cavern closed for a short time in 1966 while it was converted into a disco and licensed bar. It closed for good in May 1973 when it was demolished to allow for the construction of the underground railway that is now the city's Northern Line. Early in the 1980s the club was partly rebuilt. The original archways were found to have been only filled with rubble and were restored. It is now a live music venue and disco.

On the wall almost opposite is a life-sized bronze model of John Lennon and the Cavern Wall of Fame, made of bricks inscribed with the names of all the groups that appeared at the original club between 1957 and 1973. The Wall of Fame was unveiled by Gerry Marsden, of the group Gerry and the Pacemakers, in 1997.

Close by is a collection of Gold Disc replicas, giving the names of all those who have had number ones in the charts between 1953 (Lita Roza) and 2002 (Atomic Kitten). This was unveiled in 2001 by Lita Roza and the Lord Mayor of Liverpool.

On Stanley Street nearby is a statue of 'Eleanor Rigby', the subject of the Beatles song of the same name, which was sculpted by the singer Tommy Steele in 1982.

A FLOOR THAT IS RARELY UNVEILED

St George's Hall, Lime Street

Access

On Lime Street.

St George's Hall, one of the most prominent and notable buildings of the city, was started in 1838, but not finished until 1854. Built at a cost of £400,000, it was designed by Harvey Lonsdale Elmes, who was aged only twenty-four when his design was accepted after a competition. Unfortunately he died of tuberculosis in 1847 while construction was under way. For the next four years construction continued under Sir Robert Rawlinson, and it was finally to be completed under C.R. Cockerell, whose main responsibility was its final decoration.

The completed building has over 7 miles of underfloor pipes for ventilation purposes. The south portico has eight Corinthian columns, which support stone sculptures by Cockerell within its pediments. It has been described as 'not only the best Greco-Roman building in Europe, but representing the climax of a long movement'. Certainly, the originality of its design and the quality of its decorative detail are very fine.

The building is 400ft long, and comprises a main hall, some 51ft long and 73ft wide, with a barrel-vaulted roof. There is a large 'Father Willis' organ, which is not part of the original Elmes design, and an elaborately designed floor with some 20,000 encaustic brown and blue Minton tiles brought from the Potteries. To preserve the appearance of the tiles, the floor is kept covered with a wooden surface and is only shown to the public every few years. Its uncovering in 1987 was only the eighth time in the twentieth century.

There are smaller areas at each end of the main hall which were used as Assize Courts until the early 1980s, and there is a smaller concert hall at first-floor level. In recent years the building has not been used much, except for the occasional organ recital and trade exhibition. An £18 million major refurbishment was completed in 2005.

Close by is Liverpool's Wellington Column, built in 1863, an exact copy of the Melville Monument in Edinburgh. At the top of William Brown Street are the city's 'standard measures' showing distances in feet measured at a temperature of 62 degrees Fahrenheit.

'DICKIE LEWIS'

Liverpool Resurgent, *Lewis's department store*

Access

Above the entrance to Lewis's at the Lime Street, Renshaw Street and Ranelagh Street junction.

This 18ft high statue dates from 1956 and is by the famous twentieth-century sculptor, Jacob Epstein. Lewis's department store (now the only store in the group, which is not to be confused with those of the John Lewis Partnership), was bombed in the blitz, but was later rebuilt in the postwar years.

The main entrance on the prominent street corner was to have been concave, but the design was altered to accommodate the statue, positioned on top of another work showing a ship's prow with figures. The whole work was intended to symbolise the struggle and determination of the city to rehabilitate itself after the grim and destructive war years.

The original design was to have incorporated a family group, but the design was subsequently changed. Epstein himself gave the statue an alternative name, *Adventurous Youth*.

When first unveiled, there was a murmur of approval, but some described it as the 'demon from hell', in view of its explicit, if slightly under-endowed, content.

A local councillor at the time dismissed these suggestions, saying that the complainants would come to accept the statue, just as they had accepted similar carvings on St George's Hall. He was proved right, and the statue has been affectionately known as 'Dickie Lewis' for some time now.

An Unusual Letter Box

Letter Box, Copperas Street

Located in a
small enclosure
off the south
side of Copperas
Street, in front of
the Royal Mail
Sorting Office.

This unusual and ornate letter box (it is not technically correct to call them post-boxes) is a Liverpool 'Special' (design PB5/2), cast in 1863 by Cochrane & Company of Dudley. It was introduced so that the Post Office could deal with the special and heavy posting requirements found in certain parts of the city. It differed from standard boxes as it had a large crown on the top and had the lettering 'Post Office' embossed below the aperture. A mail bag could also be hung inside.

According to a plaque on the box it was originally located in Everton and was withdrawn from service in September 1978. Close by is a small war memorial to the men from the former Northern Delivery Office on Walton Road who died in the First World War. It was relocated here in 1991.

Another example of the Liverpool 'Special' box can be found at the Albert Dock, outside the Atlantic Pavilion. Other historic letter boxes can be found at Abercrombie Square in the University, at Dingle, Stanley and in the Woolton Park area.

A LITTLE-KNOWN *TITANIC MEMORIAL*

Titanic *Band Memorial, Philharmonic Hall*

This plaque celebrates the bandsmen who played on the ill-fated liner in 1912, best remembered in Hollywood films for their final performance on the ship's deck, which was of the hymn 'Nearer, my God, to Thee'. None of the band members survived the tragedy. *Titanic* did not set sail from Liverpool, but the viola player in the band, Fred Clarke, was from the city, and had played in the Philharmonic Hall on a few occasions, although he had not been a member of the city's Philharmonic Orchestra.

The plaque was the idea of Liverpool stockbroker, Henry Rensburg, who was also a director of the Philharmonic Society. It was dedicated on 4 November 1912. Earlier in the year the orchestra had played a benefit concert for Clarke's wife and sister, who both lived in Liverpool. The plaque correctly describes the band as passengers; they were never the official band of the ship, as is commonly believed.

The original Philharmonic Hall, dating from 1849, was destroyed by fire in 1933, although the plaque was saved. The current and replacement building, designed by Herbert Rowse, was completed in 1939. The plaque was placed in a corridor near the hall's Green Room, but it was not visible to the public. This was rectified in 1995 when the plaque was moved to its current location as part of the extensive restoration of the building completed that year.

Access

Located within the foyer of the Philharmonic Hall on Hope Street, and accessible only when the hall is open for concerts or ticket sales.

THE MOST ORNATE PUB IN ENGLAND

The Philharmonic Dining Rooms, Hope Street

Access

At the junction
of Hope Street
and Hardman
Street, diagonally
opposite the
Philharmonic
Hall.

This pub, affectionately called 'the Phil', is one of the landmarks of Liverpool. It has been called 'the most ornate pub in England' and 'the most lavish pub in Britain'. It is deservedly a Grade I listed building. Commissioned by the brewery Robert Cain & Sons, it was designed by brewery architect Walter Thomas and was built between 1898 and 1900. Robert Cain clearly intended that it would be a showpiece pub, built to resemble a gentlemen's club, and designed to appeal to the well-to-do patrons of the Philharmonic Hall.

Inside, the Phil has dark wooden panels, copper bas-reliefs, mosaic floors, Art Nouveau light fittings and stained-glass windows commemorating the Boer War heroes Baden Powell and Earl Roberts. The main bar is decorated with stained glass, bunches of glass grapes and a large golden eagle, which keeps an eye on proceedings. There are three rooms off the main bar, a smoke room called Brahms, the Liszt (which is a no-smoking newsroom) and the Grand Lounge, originally a billiard room but now used as a restaurant.

The Grand Lounge is decorated with ornate chandeliers, stained-glass skylights, a magnificent ceiling and an elaborately carved fireplace called *The Murmur of the Sea* (showing Apollo with two female companions). A decorative plaster frieze runs around the room.

Upstairs are two large rooms originally used as restaurants but now used for special functions, along with facilities for waiting coachmen. The gents' toilets are legendary and have elaborate marble wash basins, copper taps and elaborate glazed urinals (women can view the toilets with permission).

John Lennon complained that one of the downsides to fame was 'not going to the Phil any more'.

An Unusual Memorial to an Avid Gambler

W. McKenzie's tombstone, St Andrew's churchyard

Access

Located on the northern side of Rodney Street. Public access into the churchyard is not currently possible.

This 15ft pyramid-shaped tombstone, dating from 1868, commemorates W. McKenzie, a nineteenth-century railway contractor and keen gambler. McKenzie wished to be buried standing upright at a card table holding the winning hand, and the result is this vertical tomb.

The adjoining St Andrew's Church, of which now only the shell remains, was built between 1824 and 1825 to the design of John Foster Jnr. Its construction was aided with financial support from the Laird family of shipbuilders and iron founders, and it was a Church of Scotland church. It closed in the 1970s and was destroyed by a serious fire in 1983. The site was subsequently sold with a view to developing it as medical consulting rooms, but little work has been done since. In early 2004 Liverpool City Council was reported as initiating a compulsory purchase order so that restoration of the building could progress.

Further along Rodney Street, at no. 62, is an elegant Georgian house that was the birthplace of W.A. Gladstone, four times Prime Minister of Britain, and sometimes described as 'Liverpool's Greatest Son'.

LIVERPOOL'S 'BLITZ' CHURCH

St Luke's Church, Leece Street

Access

At the bottom end of Leece Street, at the junction with Berry Street.

This church, designed by John Foster Snr in 1802, was redesigned and completed by his son John Foster Jnr in 1831. Built in the perpendicular Gothic style, it was noted for its decorated pinnacles and traceried windows.

It was bombed in the blitz of May 1941 and was never restored, being left as a shell to signify the horrors of war. The City Council purchased it in 1968 and the grounds have been laid out as public gardens. There is a modern memorial column (1998) by Eamonn O'Docherty to the Irish Famine of 1845 to 1852, and a memorial to the entertainer Roy Castle, who came from the city. Recently, proposals have been made to restore a peel of church bells to the old tower.

See nearby, on Nelson Street, the 44ft high Chinese Arch, at the heart of Liverpool's Chinatown, said to be the oldest Chinese community in Europe. Built in 2000 at a cost of £220,000, the arch was erected by a team of workmen from Shanghai in just ninety days. It is elaborately decorated with 200 hand-carved Chinese dragons, 188 traditional dragons and 12 pregnant dragons. The arch symbolises good fortune, harmony and growth.

IS IT A FRUIT OR AN ANIMAL?

Superlamb Banana

Access

On Tithebarn
Street, next to
the John Moores
University
building.

This 7½ tonne piece of bright yellow modern art first appeared in Liverpool in May 1998 when it was unveiled on the waterfront as part of Arttranspennine '98. It blends the head of a lamb into a banana. Designed by Japanese artist Taro Chieso, it cost £35,000 and was designed to warn of the dangers of genetic engineering and also to symbolise the playful spirit of the city.

Local opinion was mostly in favour of the unusual sculpture, but there were some objections. After being in its initial location for a few months it then spent some time in Williamson Square. Next it was moved to the waterfront at Wapping in front of the building featuring old signs for the Joseph Lamb Company. In October 2002 it was painted pink for a time to publicise Breast Cancer Awareness month. In early May 2005 it moved to its curent location. It now seems to have been accepted as part of the Liverpool landscape, and has recently acquired 'Capital of Culture' decoration.

Close by, also on the frontage, is Chavasse Park, named after Noel Chavasse (1884–1917), one of only three servicemen to have been awarded the Victoria Cross twice. His father was at one time Bishop of Liverpool. The park until recently contained the Yellow Submarine, from the Beatles' song of the same name, which was on display at the Liverpool Garden Festival in 1984/5.

On Park Lane is the 'Swedish church', or the Gustav Adolph church, built in 1883 for Scandinavian seamen visiting the port. The flags of all the Scandinavian countries can normally be seen flying outside it, and it now incorporates the local Swedish Consulate.

ONE OF THE GREAT BUILDINGS OF THE TWENTIETH CENTURY

Liverpool Anglican Cathedral

Access

Via Cathedral Gates, off Upper Duke Street.

Liverpool Cathedral is the largest Anglican Cathedral in Britain. It was built in local sandstone (from Woolton) over a period of seventy-four years, being finally dedicated by the Queen in 1978. The foundation stone, the heaviest in the building at some 4 tons, was dedicated by King Edward VII in 1904. The cathedral was designed by Sir Giles Gilbert Scott, who also designed buildings as diverse as the former Battersea power station and the old red telephone box. The decision to appoint him architect was a surprising one at the time, for he was only twenty-two and a Roman Catholic.

The building is perhaps the final manifestation of the Gothic style of cathedral construction in Britain. The sheer height of the building is overwhelming. Originally there were to have been two towers, but this was changed in 1910 to a 321ft high single tower, called the Vestey Tower after its benefactor. There are two lifts or 108 steps to the top. The bells are the highest in the country, at 200ft above floor level and the largest bell, 'Great George', weighs nearly 15 tons.

Unlike most cathedrals, there is no central screen to block the view from the west end right through to the sanctuary. There is impressive statuary both inside and outside the building, stained glass, paintings and a collection of ecclesiastical embroidery in the Elisabeth Hoare Gallery. The main organ in the cathedral, built by Father Willis between 1923 and 1926, has two consoles, five manuals (keyboards) and is the largest pipe organ in Britain.

LIVERPOOL'S HIDDEN PARK

St James's Park

This fascinating park is formed out of an old quarry, the stone from which was used in many public buildings in the city and docks from the sixteenth to the early nineteenth centuries. Its original use as a quarry means that the park is at a considerably lower level than the surrounding streets, and is not widely known even to long-standing residents of the city. The park is about 90yds wide, and about 500yds long.

Quarrying had ceased by 1825, and between 1827 and 1829 it was laid out as a public cemetery by the town council, using the services of the architect John Foster (1786–1846). He was instructed to lay it out along the lines of the Père-Lachaise cemetery in Paris. The result is a unique urban location of surprising dramatic grandeur. The main entrance runs through a tunnel that leads down to the burial ground, which is laid out with winding paths and generously provided with trees.

Access

Either via the footpath which leads to the left of the entrance to the cathedral or via the gate at the junction of St James's Road and Upper Parliament Street.

In the centre is the impressive Huskisson memorial, commemorating the MP who died when the Liverpool and Manchester Railway first opened (see page 120). On the eastern wall is a spring, first noted in 1773, at one time referred to as the Liverpool Spa in view of its supposed curative properties. In the far northern corner is the entrance to a disused tunnel, formerly used as a means of access by hearses. Close to this is another tunnel, which appears to burrow under the cathedral and which dates from the time of the quarry.

The last burial in the cemetery was in 1936. It remained unused and overgrown until 1972 when the council restored it as a public park. Although its hidden nature encourages vandalism, fortunately attention is once again being given to this 'little gem' of a park. The earlier photograph shows the site in 1936, with continuing construction work on the cathedral behind.

A MYSTERIOUS NEO-CLASSICAL BUILDING

Oratory, St James's Cemetery

Access

Via Cathedral
Gate, off Upper
Duke Street.

Immediately adjoining the tunnel entrance to St James's Park is the Oratory, the former chapel of St James's Cemetery. Also designed by John Foster, the foundation stone of the Greek Revival building was laid in September 1827 by the Rector of Liverpool. The Oratory allowed funeral services to be conducted on site prior to burials taking place in the cemetery. It also contains several fine monuments to the deceased.

The building is simply laid out and was small enough to allow it to be lit solely by means of a skylight. Consequently there are no windows in the building, which adds to its mystery. The Oratory fell into disuse when the cemetery closed in 1936. The adjoining cathedral authorities looked after it until 1980 when it was handed over to Merseyside County Council. Responsibility now rests with the National Museums and Galleries on Merseyside. It is not normally open to the public.

ONCE KNOWN AS FALKNER'S FOLLY

Access

Off Grove Street.

Falkner Square

This square is one of the earliest public open spaces in Liverpool and is often likened to many of London's Georgian squares for its elegance. It is named after Edward Falkner of Fairfield, who was born in 1760. Falkner had enjoyed a meteoric career in the Army, and at the age of twenty-eight was appointed Sheriff of Lancashire. In 1797, when England was threatened with an invasion by the French, it is said that he managed to raise a local fighting force of 1,000 men within twenty-four hours.

In his later years Falkner invested in land and property, with Falkner Square being completed in 1830. Many of the handsome houses stood empty for years as the square was too far out of town, and transport up the hill was difficult in the days of horse and carriage. The square became known as Falkner's Folly for a time, and the gardens were taken over by the local authority as early as 1835. With the expansion of the town, the square eventually became fashionable.

Over the years the gardens deteriorated, and during the Second World War were used as the site of air raid shelters. In the 1950s the gardens were restored, although they continued to be a private 'key garden', accessible only to surrounding residents. Recently the gardens have been restored again, and are now freely accessible to the public, having been awarded Green Flag status in 2003.

NAMED AFTER A REMARKABLE LANDLORD

Peter Kavanagh's, Egerton Street

Access

Located near the western end of Egerton Street.

The location of this pub could be regarded as unique. Lying on the border between the University and Toxteth, it attracts custom from both areas, which creates a rich mix of clientele.

Built in the nineteenth century, it was taken over by Peter Kavanagh in the 1890s, and still retains its original layout, although in the past it has been extended to take in adjoining property. Kavanagh named it The Grapes. He was a well-known character in Liverpool and served as a city councillor for a time. The pub features some of his own inventions, such as the tables in the two semi-circular snugs, which were fitted with locking features so that they could be used on ocean liners. These same snugs also feature murals by the Edinburgh-born artist Eric Robertson (1887–1941), which were painted in 1929 when Kavanagh was altering the pub. One of the snugs is 'no smoking', until recently fairly rare in a public house.

The chief feature of the establishment is the huge collection of bric-a-brac which hangs from the ceilings. This collection, which includes old radios, bicycles, model cars and an old alligator skin, was started by Kavanagh and has been added to since his death in 1950, by which time the pub bore his name.

A CATHOLIC CATHEDRAL DESIGNED BY A PROTESTANT

Access

Via Mount
Pleasant or
Brownlow Hill.

Metropolitan Cathedral of Christ the King

Not long after the establishment of the Catholic Diocese of Liverpool in 1850 thoughts turned to the building of a Catholic cathedral. Edward Welby Pugin, son of A.W. Pugin (designer of the Houses of Commons), was commissioned, and by 1856 a usable building in the form of a Lady Chapel had been built on a site in Everton.

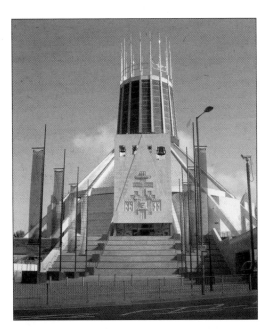

Lack of funds brought a halt to the work, but in 1922 the idea of a cathedral was resurrected. Money began to be raised and in 1930 the site of the former Poor Law Workhouse on Brownlow Hill was purchased. Sir Edwin Lutyens, the noted architect of the Whitehall Cenotaph and New Delhi, was employed. The central feature of his design was to have been a huge dome, based on that of St Peter's in Rome, with a height of some 520ft. Work started in 1933 on the crypt of the new building, but it was suspended at the outbreak of the Second World War, and was only completed in the 1950s.

In the meantime it had been realised that the original Lutyens scheme would have been far too costly, so it was scaled down. In 1960 it was abandoned when a worldwide competition was launched to find a new design. The requirement was for a building to hold 3,000 which could be completed within ten years. The competition was won by Sir Frederick Gibberd (1908–84), a Protestant. Work started in October 1962 and was completed in May 1967. The building is effectively built on top of the Lutyens crypt.

The Gibberd building is a circular conical structure with a central high altar, a rectangular block of white marble from the former Yugoslavia, above which is a cylinder of stained glass with a filigree of the Crown of Thorns. The cathedral is affectionately (or denigratingly) known in the area as either 'Paddy's Wigwam' or the 'Mersey Funnel'. The effect of the stained glass is impressive, either from inside the building during the day, or at night from the outside, when the stained glass glows from the lights within. In recent years the building has been extensively restored, as faults due to certain aspects of the 1960s construction were appearing.

CLOCK DESIGNED AS AN AID TO SHIPPING

Victoria Tower, Salisbury Dock

This tower is another feature of the Liverpool docks designed by its famous engineer Jesse Hartley, docks engineer from 1824 to 1860. In all he was responsible for building some sixteen docks and his buildings were all designed to last.

Victoria Tower, sometimes called the 'Dockers Clock', was built in 1848. It is a unique six-sided clock provided as an aid to ships' captains to help them set the correct time on the ships' chronometers when leaving the port. It also contained a bell to signal high tide, fog and other warnings.

The tower is built of irregularly shaped blocks of granite. It has a high, tapered, circular base pierced with rounded arch openings. The top is a projecting castellated parapet carried on corbels. The clock has not been kept in working order for some time now.

Access

This is best seen from the river on the Mersey Ferries Explorer Tours. Access can sometimes be gained via gates on the western side of Regent Road (A5036), but visitors should be aware that the docks are private property, and that semi-derelict docks are dangerous places.

THE LARGEST BRICK WAREHOUSE IN THE WORLD

Tobacco Warehouse, Stanley Dock

Access

Visible from the lift bridge which carried Regent Road over the Stanley Dock branch of the Leeds and Liverpool Canal.

This warehouse was built in 1900 and was the biggest building in the world at the time. Even today it is said to be the largest ever brick building. It is 125ft high, has fourteen storeys and some 36 acres of floorspace. Some 27 million bricks and 6,000 tons of iron were used in its construction. The upper floors were designed to be fireproof.

The building had to be big, as tobacco is a seasonal crop and enough space was needed to be able to store a whole year's supplies for the market. During the Second World War it was used as a supply depot by the American Army, and was visited by Eleanor Roosevelt, wife of the US President, in 1942. It has not been used as a tobacco warehouse since the 1980s, but a weekly Sunday market is held on the ground floor.

A Tower Depicted on the Crest of Everton Football Club

Everton Beacon

Access

On the eastern side of Netherfield Road South.

This small round tower was built as a bridewell or lock-up in 1787. Its current local name is a misnomer, as the original Everton Beacon, shown in the illustration below, stood over half a mile to the north near the junction of Beacon Lane and St Domingo Road. It had been built by Ranulf, Earl of Chester, in about 1230 and was used to guide ships travelling up the Mersey estuary to Liverpool. It was a plain, square two-storey building, with a guardroom upstairs and a kitchen on the ground floor. It is said to have blown down in a storm in 1802, so the Beacon title then passed to the old lock-up.

The Beacon has several other names, including the Round-house, Stewbum's Palace, the Stone Jug and Prince Rupert's Tower or Castle. The latter comes from the fact that Prince Rupert is reported to have used the old Beacon as a vantage point overlooking the town during the Civil War.

The tower has been used on the heraldic crest of Everton Football Club since the 1937/38 season, when it was first used on the club tie at the instigation of Theo Kelly, the club secretary. Since 1980 it has appeared on Everton shirts. The club's current supporters' shop, built in recent years on Walton Lane, incorporates the tower's shape as a corner feature of the building. Today the Everton Beacon is used by council workers to store tools. It was restored in 1997 at a cost of £15,000.

An Everton fan in the United States has built an exact replica of the Beacon in his garden.

Everton Football Club is known by the nickname the Toffees. The most favoured story for the original of the name is that their original ground was close to Ye Ancient Everton Toffee House operated by Old Ma Bushell, which was close to the Beacon. The club later moved to Anfield and then, in 1893, to the present Goodison Park, where another toffee shop was operated by Old Mother Nobletts. To avoid competition with Ma Bushell, Mrs Nobletts produced Everton Mints, which are well known to this day. Ma Bushell responded by persuading her good-looking granddaughter to distribute her toffees inside the ground on match days. This has led to the tradition of the Everton Toffee Lady, whereby before each match a different teenage girl is selected from club supporters to perform this time-honoured task.

A RELIC FROM BRUNEL'S *GREAT EASTERN*

Great Eastern *flagpole, Anfield*

Access

On the Breck
Road side of
Liverpool
Football Club's
Anfield ground,
in the corner of
the Kop and the
Kemlyn Road
stands.

The last great work of Isambard Kingdom Brunel, the Victorian railway and steamship designer and promoter, was the steamship *Great Eastern*, which first set sail in 1859. The construction of the ship had involved great problems for Brunel, which contributed to his untimely death that year. It was at the time by far the biggest ship ever constructed, powered by both propellers and paddlewheels, with auxiliary sails, and with enough coal-carrying capacity to travel to Australia and back. The *Great Eastern* was not a success as a passenger liner, and by 1865 it was being used to lay the first transatlantic telegraph cable, in which use it continued for another fifteen or so years.

By the 1880s the ship was lying off Wirral. During the Liverpool Exhibition of 1887 it was being used as a floating advertisement hoarding for Lewis's department store. At the same time it also housed a funfair and dance hall,

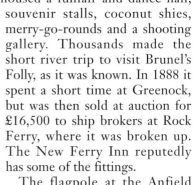

souvenir stalls, coconut shies, merry-go-rounds and a shooting gallery. Thousands made the short river trip to visit Brunel's Folly, as it was known. In 1888 it spent a short time at Greenock, but was then sold at auction for £16,500 to ship brokers at Rock Ferry, where it was broken up. The New Ferry Inn reputedly has some of the fittings.

The flagpole at the Anfield ground is one of these fittings. It was floated across the Mersey and pulled up the Everton Valley by a team of four horses to be erected here in 1928 when the two adjoining stands were extended.

A MEMORIAL TO A GREAT FOOTBALL MANAGER

Shankly Gates, Liverpool Football Ground

Access

On the western side of Anfield Road.

These gates stand as a permanent tribute to Bill Shankly, the great manager of Liverpool Football Club from 1959 to 1974, who had during his term transformed the club from a struggling Second Division side into top league material.

The gates were formally unlocked by his widow, Nessie, on 26 August 1982. Across the gates are the words 'You'll Never Walk Alone', a song from the Rogers and Hammerstein musical *Carousel* that was popularised by local group Gerry and the Pacemakers in the 1960s. The song became the club's anthem after it had been played before matches a few times.

Close by is the Hillsborough Memorial, with its eternal gas flame, to the ninety-six Liverpool fans of all ages, who lost their lives during the FA Cup Semi-Final against Nottingham Forest played at the Sheffield ground on 15 April 1989. The memorial was unveiled on the first anniversary of the tragedy.

A statue of Bill Shankly by Tom Murphy, erected in 1997, stands at the Breck Road side of the ground by the supporters' shop. Another set of gates commemorates Bob Paisley, Bill Shankly's successor.

WHERE LOCAL JUSTICE WAS METED OUT

Old Court House, West Derby

Access

On the northern side of the West Derby village green, near the junction of Town Row and Mill Lane.

This simple court house, built of red sandstone, with a stone roof and mullioned windows, dates from 1662. It would have been the manorial court from the time when copyholders and other tenants were called upon to pay their dues to the lord of the manor through his steward. The manorial court derived from the feudal Wapentake courts (the regional terms for Hundred courts), and also dealt with disputes between tenants. The Wapentake court last met here in about 1825,

but the manorial court continued to meet twice yearly until 1910. The court house also held local records; these were kept in the Town Chest, which had many different locks. Only when all the keyholders were present could the chest be opened.

The court house was under threat of demolition in 1921. It was saved when a group of trustees took a lease of the building at *2s 6d* a year from Lord Salisbury. The building passed into the ownership of Liverpool Corporation in 1933, and was declared an Ancient Monument in 1935. In 1984 some of the local children re-enacted manorial court proceedings from the seventeenth century. Inside the building wooden court room furniture and a high chair for the steward of the court can be seen.

Across the road, set back from the pavement in the old pound (where stray animals were kept after market days until their owners paid the relevant fines), are the old West Derby Stocks. Originally made of wood, they were replaced by this set, made in the United States in 1801, and placed to the west of the court house. After falling into disuse they spent some time in the back garden of a Dr Wilkie, where they eventually became overgrown. They were placed on the present site in commemoration of Queen Victoria's Diamond Jubilee.

Also across the road is the white stone drinking fountain, now no longer operational, which was the gift of Liverpool councillor and petroleum broker Richard Meade-King of Broomfield in 1894. It bears the simple inscription 'Water is best', which was either an exhortation to abstention, or a subtle joke based on the fact that it stands centrally between three local public houses. An ornamental lamp, now incomplete, stands on its top.

THE SET OF A SOAP OPERA

Brookside *location, West Derby*

Access

Off the northern side of Deysbrook Lane.

This street of ordinary-looking modern houses was partly used as the set of the soap opera *Brookside*, which started in 1982, when Channel 4 was launched.

Produced by Mersey TV, *Brookside* was not filmed in a studio but used six of the houses on the estate. A total of thirteen houses were bought for the series by producer Phil Redmond; the others were used for make-up, wardrobe and the staff canteen. Not all the houses on the estate were bought for the soap those that remained were separated by a barrier and security hut which prevented public access.

Brookside was originally to have been called *Meadowcroft*. It differed from other soap operas on offer at the time by showing a realism that tackled the social and political problems of the day. The use of hand-held cameras added to this realism. A Saturday omnibus edition led the way for others in the genre to follow. It also differed from other soaps by not having a central focal point, such as a corner shop or public house.

Over the years *Brookside* proved controversial, but in its later years its tone became more mainstream, showing similarities to the more upmarket Chester-based *Hollyoaks*, also made by Mersey TV. After a drop in the ratings it was taken off the air by Channel 4 in November 2003.

A VILLAGE WITH STREETS NAMED AFTER THE INGREDIENTS OF JAM

Hartley Village

Access

To the west of
Long Lane
(B5187), via
Hartley Avenue.

William Pickles Hartley (1846–1922) was born in Colne, and began life as a grocer. After a supplier failed to deliver some jam he made his own, and was soon in production. He founded a factory at Bootle, but soon had to move to a larger site at Aintree, with improved rail access, so vital for the delivery of fresh ingredients. The new factory opened in 1886 and was designed in red brick to look like a medieval castle, with an impressive castellated gateway. A tall brick clock tower stood in the centre of the complex.

Hartley was an enlightened employer and provided a pension scheme, generous wages, profit sharing and a company doctor for his employees. For the nucleus of skilled key workers he built Hartley Village in 1888. Designed by Sugden & Sons of Leek who had won an architectural competition, it is a modest scheme when compared with other philanthropic ones of the late nineteenth century, providing only forty-nine houses. However, the streets were wide and a minimum 12ft wide passageway was provided behind the houses. Most of the houses were rented at between *2s 6d* and *3s 6d* a week, although some were available for sale on twenty-year mortgages at low rates of interest.

Many of the houses were grouped round a central 1-acre bowling green, now alas a car park. The streets are all named after the ingredients of jam – Sugar Street, Spice Street, Red Currant Court, Cherry Row, etc. Tennis courts were built and a pond was stocked with fish. The Hartley name and monogram are much in evidence. Writing in 1888, *The Builder* magazine reported '[the architects] have designed the cottages in conformity with the old domestic buildings indigenous to the district and avoiding all flimsy and supposed "picturesque" ornamental additions – for which they are entirely to be commended'.

The factory proved very profitable, and expanded substantially in 1891, 1899 and 1923. More houses were either bought or built for employees, including some on nearby Cedar Road, bringing the total to seventy-one. Funds were provided for the building of the Aintree Primitive Methodist Chapel and a temperance hotel, the Aintree Institute, which was built in 1896.

Hartley's was taken over by Schweppes in 1959, and the Aintree factory closed in the 1970s, when the clock tower was demolished. The factory has now been divided up as a trading estate, and the village now looks rather down-at-heel. It is not a Conservation Area. The largest house, Inglewood, has been demolished.

A SERIES OF TUNNELS BUILT FOR NO APPARENT PURPOSE

Williamson Tunnels

Access

The Williamson Tunnels Heritage Centre is on Smithdown Lane, opposite the traffic police building and close to the junction with Grinfield Street. It is open Tuesday to Sunday in summer and Thursday to Sunday in winter. Admission charge payable.

Joseph Williamson, born in 1769, moved to Liverpool in about 1780 and in the years that followed built up a lucrative tobacco business, partly through his involvement with the firm of Richard Tate. In 1805 Williamson moved with his wife into an existing house on Mason Street and promptly set about building more properties on the street. As the houses were located on a rocky outcrop, caused by earlier quarrying, Williamson decided that the houses needed larger gardens. The only way this could be achieved would be by building archways at the lower level on Smithdown Lane. The arches thus created became the starting point of his tunnel system.

In the years until his death in 1840 Williamson employed labourers who excavated a mysterious system of tunnels under the surrounding area. They are all shapes, sizes and levels ranging from just a few feet to 25ft in width in the so-called 'Banqueting Hall'. There are 'tunnels upon tunnels' where one archway rises above another. The work earned him the title 'the King of Edge Hill' in the area.

The reason why Williamson built the tunnels is not known. Their design and layout precludes much logical use. The most favoured explanation is that he was employing the labourers on some sort of job creation project, perhaps in anticipation of the building of the railways. Other suggestions include possible religious use and that they represent a huge underground work of art. Williamson was secretive about the project throughout his life.

After his death in 1840 work on the system ceased, and the tunnels were abandoned, many being filled with rubble and rubbish from the rapidly expanding city. The exact extent of the system is not known, although further information is coming to light as the system is excavated further. The tunnels, however, were never completely forgotten about, and after many suggestions work on exploring and excavating the tunnels was initiated by the Joseph Williamson Society, with the first section opening to the public in autumn 2002.

BRITAIN'S FIRST BOTANICAL GARDENS

Wavertree Botanical Gardens

Access

On the south side of Edge Lane (A5047) at the junction with Botanic Road.

Liverpool was the first city to have a botanical garden. It opened on a 5-acre site near the current Myrtle Street in Mount Pleasant in 1800, several decades before London's Kew Gardens. William Roscoe, man of letters and MP for the city, was one of the leading lights in its establishment and gave the address at the official opening.

The gardens were a commercial enterprise, funded by subscriptions, and were intended to test newly discovered species for potential commercial value. Within five years it had more than 1,000 trees, shrubs and other plants, some 450 in a 240ft long greenhouse.

By 1831 the venture was in financial difficulties and in 1836 it moved to this 11-acre site, designed by John Shepherd. The curator's lodge (right), a Grade II listed building, dates from this period. In 1841 Liverpool Corporation were obliged to step in to pay off a debt of £3,800, in return for which it secured free public access on two days a week. In 1846 it bought the gardens outright.

Between 1849 and 1864 the layout was changed, creating the diagonal planting beds seen today. However, the herbaceous borders remain from the initial design. Notable visitors at the time included the sultan of Zanzibar and the mayor of Dublin. The site was also used for important exhibitions.

The gardens had lost their reputation by the end of the nineteenth century, and when the

barrel-vaulted glass houses by Robson and Tyreman (seen above) were destroyed in the Blitz of 1940 they were not replaced. The site was renamed Wavertree Park in about 1950, and work on a replacement site at Harthill next to Calderstones Park started in 1951, officially opening in 1964. The botanical collection remained at Harthill until 1984, since when it has been at Greenhill Nursery.

In recent years the Edge Lane site has again been called the Wavertree Botanical Gardens, and there are hopes that both the curator's lodge and some interesting air raid shelters from the Second World War, which still contain wall murals from the time, can be restored and opened to the public.

A VILLAGE LOCK-UP AND LIVERPOOL'S ONLY COMMON LAND

Wavertree lock-up

Access

On the grassed
area between
Lake Road, Mill
Lane and
Childwall Road,
Wavertree. It is
open to the
public during
Heritage Open
Week each
September.

This octagonal village lock-up, sometimes called the Round House, was built in 1796 of yellow sandstone, at local expense. At the time it was the village constable's job to maintain order and prevent drunkenness. Villagers took it in turns to perform this duty, which was unpaid, although they were allowed expenses of 2*s* if prisoners were kept overnight in the constable's own house.

When it was being built objections were raised by John Myers, the owner of the former Lake House, on the grounds that his view would be spoilt, but these were rejected. The building work was carried out by a Mr Hind. The completed building had a flattish roof, with parapet, and was equipped with a small stove. The parapet allowed prisoners' friends to hide and organise escapes through the roof.

The building became redundant in 1845 when Wavertree's first police station opened. The lock-up had been used in 1832 to house cholera victims and later by destitute Irish escaping the potato famine. Later it was used to store the village fire hose. By 1860 it had become derelict and in 1868 the owners, the Wavertree Board of Health, considered demolition.

The building was saved and beautified when the board's chairman, James Picton, drew up plans for its restoration, which included a pitched roof and a weather vane. Some decades ago it was given listed building status and in 1979 Wavertree Village was declared a Conservation Area. The land on which the building stands has been ascertained as the city's only piece of common land.

A Clock Built in Memory of his Wife

Picton Clock Tower

Access

At the junction of Childwall Road, High Street and Church Road North.

James Allanson Picton was a prominent citizen of Liverpool in the mid-nineteenth century. He served on both the City Council and the local Board of Health. The Picton Library in the city centre was named after him in 1879 in recognition of his forty years of service on its Libraries Committee. In 1881 he was knighted for his 'high attainments and public services'. He was also an architect and surveyor, a linguist and a keen local historian.

The clock tower was presented to Wavertree in 1884, and was a memorial to his wife of fifty years, Sarah Pooley, who had died in 1879. Sir James chose the place for his memorial well, and the landmark is so well known that it featured on the opening credits for *Brookside*. In times past, before watches were common, local parents would ask their children to 'go and see what the time is by Sarah Pooley'. It has the inscription 'Time wasted is existence, used is life'.

Close by, on the northern side of High Street, immediately to the right of the Cock and Bottle pub, is what used to be England's smallest house, 95 High Street. It was 6ft wide, 14ft deep and had two rooms. Families lived in it until 1952 when it was incorporated into the public house. One family had eight children. Another occupant was rather large and had to go up the internal staircase sideways, even after it had been widened from 8in wide to 16in. The original frontage was restored by Bass Taverns in 1998. The pub is currently closed awaiting refurbishment.

A STONE MEMORIAL TO AN OLD DISPUTE OVER WATER

Salisbury Stone, Wavertree

Access

Located in the children's playground on the western side of Mill Lane at its junction with Lake Road.

This sandstone block contains a crown and a letter 'S' on its surface. The old Wavertree Lake, sometimes called Piggy Lake, existed until 1929, when it was drained, its site now forming the children's playground. During the latter part of the nineteenth century it had become weed-infested and dirty, reflecting the increased urbanisation of the area. The local Board of Health resolved in 1861 to clean it up and surround it with trees, but its owner, the Marquess of Salisbury and lord of the manor of Wavertree, was not pleased. He ordered boundary markers, or 'mere stones', to be put around the edge of his property to delineate it from common land. Eventually the dispute was resolved and the Marquess gave way, allowing the Board to proceed with its proposals. This stone remains to remind us of the dispute.

Close by, on the western side of Mill Lane at its junction with North Drive, stands Monks' Well, which is inscribed with the Latin motto 'Qui non dat quod Habet, Doemon Infra ridet. Anno 1414', or 'He who hath and wont bestow the devil will reckon with below'. The exact age of this well is not known. It used to stand further back from the road, with steps in the archway masonry that allowed access to the stone cistern containing the water. There are stories of it being connected by underground passages to the so-called Childwall Abbey or other buildings, but these are thought to be untrue and based on the fact that an outlet channel had been constructed in the late eighteenth century to take the water closer to the nearest road. In 1834 the local authorities installed an iron pump to lift the water, but after the arrival of piped water in the 1850s it fell into disuse. It was presented to Liverpool Corporation in the 1930s and became one of the city's first listed buildings in 1952.

A HOUSE NAMED AFTER SIR WALTER SCOTT'S BIRTHPLACE

Sandy Knowe, Wavertree

This large red sandstone house stands at the highest point of Olive Mount, some 215ft above sea level. It was built in 1847 by James Picton. Among his many interests and achievements Picton was a literary scholar and traveller. Picton named his house after the farm where Sir Walter Scott was brought up. There is in fact a similarity between the design of the house and Smailholm Tower, an old border fortress, which is located close to Sandy Knowe Farm near Kelso in the Scottish Borders. Picton built the polygonal extension, which incorporates the family coat of arms, to house his private library. He died here in 1889.

The house was used for many years as an Independent Methodist chapel, but in 1975 it was converted by Merseyside Improved Homes to form sheltered flats. These are currently administered by the Riverside Housing Association.

Access

On the western side of Mill Lane, at the junction with Long Lane.

LIVERPOOL'S GARDEN SUBURB

Access

At the eastern
end of Thingwall
Road.

Wavertree Garden Suburb

Wavertree Garden Suburb was built by Liverpool Garden Suburb Tenants Ltd, a company in which all the houses were owned collectively and where the tenants were the shareholders of the company. It was one of a number of similar developments being planned at the time along the 'garden city' lines advocated by Ebenezer Howard at Letchworth.

Work on the first phase of the scheme started in July 1910 to a design by Howard's associate, Raymond Unwin, the first house being 13 Wavertree Nook Road, then called Paxway. By the end of 1914, when construction work ceased, some 360 houses had been completed, out of the 1,800 originally planned.

The housing density of the estate was deliberately set low, at only eleven houses to the acre, considerably fewer than surrounding developments. The architecture of the estate has a distinctly 'cottagey' feel, with wide grass verges, natural features and hedges, rather than fences. A large Institute for residents was planned for a site on Queens Drive, but did not materialise because of the First World War. Instead, two cottages on Thingwall Road, pictured here, which had been used since 1912, became the permanent home of the Institute, which still functions today. A residents' newspaper, the *Thingwallian*, was produced.

The introduction of rent controls during the First World War made the finances of the estate company difficult, and many of the houses were sold off to tenants in the 1930s, with the remaining undeveloped land going to speculative builders. The company itself was wound up in 1938. The tennis courts, bowling greens and Institute were all transferred to a charitable trust. The suburb was made a Conservation Area in 1971.

LIVERPOOL'S OLDEST CHURCH

All Saints' Church, Childwall

Access

At the junction
of Childwall
Abbey Road,
Childwall Lane
and Score Lane.

All Saints' is Liverpool's only remaining medieval church. It was formerly known as St Peter's. Its aisles date from the fourteenth and fifteenth centuries. The church's list of births, marriages and deaths dates from 1557 and runs to the end of the eighteenth century. The oldest graves in the churchyard date from 1620 to 1686, and the squire's pew dates from 1740. The tower was rebuilt in 1810 and the chancel floor was raised 3ft in 1851. In 1906 the northern side of the church was rebuilt.

The interior of the church is well worth a visit. There is also a lychgate and the hearse house, used for housing the horse-drawn village hearse in the days before commercial undertakers became common; it can be seen on the left of the photograph.

The battlemented public house on the opposite side of the road is called the Childwall Abbey. The name of the pub is somewhat of a misnomer as it is now felt that there never was an abbey at Childwall, only a chantry, where masses for the dead were said. The field adjoining the church on the northern side is called 'Bloody Acre' and is said to be the site of a battle during the Civil War.

ANCIENT STONES WHICH HAVE GIVEN THEIR NAME TO A PARK

The Calderstones, Calderstones Park

Access

In the northern quarter of the park. The nearest entrance is at the junction of Harthill Road and Calderstones Road. If the greenhouse is not open, the park rangers' office in the centre of the park can sometimes arrange for access.

These six stones, believed to date from the late Neolithic or early Bronze Ages, are placed in a random order inside a small ornamental greenhouse. They are thought to be the remains of a tomb that stood in an earth mound at a crossroads in Allerton. W.A. Herdman, the noted local writer, recorded in 1896 that they had been found within the mound, along with clay urns and many burnt bones, when the road now known as Menlove Avenue was being widened in 1789. This, together with the fact that the stones appeared to have been some form of hut or cellar, indicated beyond doubt that it was an ancient burial site. An artist's impression is thought to show the site in about 1840.

In 1845 Joseph Walker placed the stones in a new position inside a low circular wall (which is still there) next to one of the park's entrances opposite Druid's Cross Road. They remained there until 1954 when they were removed for cleaning and preservation. Ten years later they were placed in their present site at what was then the entrance to the city's Botanical Gardens in the former Harthill greenhouses.

The stones are of local sandstone and vary from 3ft to 8ft in height. They are badly worn, but many of the original carvings are visible. These are a variety of spirals, concentric rings, arcs, cup and ring marks and representations of human feet. The latter are unusual in that they have six toes. There are also more modern carvings visible, including Victorian boot shapes and twentieth-century graffiti.

The style of the carvings and the supposed design of the tomb is comparatively rare. Similar tombs have been found in Ireland and on two sites in Anglesey. One of the stones, in both spiral carvings and shape, is similar to Long Meg in Cumbria.

A FORTOTTEN MEMORIAL TO THE CITY'S MOST FAMOUS DOCK ENGINEER

Hartley Pillar, Calderstones Park

This almost-forgotten 10ft high pillar is a shaft of Scottish grey granite sent as a specimen to Jesse Hartley, when he was engineer to the Liverpool Docks. It clearly shows measurements cut into it for demonstration purposes.

The pillar originally stood over Hartley's grave in Crosby churchyard. In the late nineteenth century it was erected by John Bibby, Hartley's son-in-law, on the lawn of Harthill, the large house that had been built on the site in 1825. However, Harthill was demolished in the late 1930s and the lawn has become a little overgrown. Recently, suggestions have been made to move the pillar to a more prominent setting, but nothing has come of this yet.

Access

Located in the hedge dividing the park from the former Harthill greenhouses site, a few yards to the right of the greenhouse containing the Calderstones.

At the Harthill entrance to the park, formerly the entrance to Harthill, is an ornate gateway containing two figures representing the god Atlantis, together with four carved maidens representing the seasons. These were originally located on a building built in 1861 adjoining Liverpool Town Hall, and were carved by Edwin Stirling. When the building was demolished in 1928 Liverpool Corporation took over the statues and placed them on pedestals at the park entrance. Some locals at the time objected to women standing around on street corners, and the statues were daubed with paint in 1937 and 1945, but, thankfully, never since.

ALLERTON'S 'LAW OAK'

Allerton Oak, Calderstones Park

Access

On the eastern side of the park, close to the Calderstones Road/Menlove Avenue junction.

This ancient oak is believed to be about 700 or 1,000 years old. Like many old trees of its type, the central trunk has divided and 'hollowed out' over the years and its spreading branches are now supported by stakes. One story is that this was caused by a ship on the River Mersey that exploded sometime during the nineteenth century, blowing out all the windows in the park's mansion house.

In medieval times the Court of the West Derby Hundred met beneath its branches, hence the name Law Oak.

Within the Old English Garden in the park is the grave and memorial to 'Jet of Iada', a black Alsatian dog, owned by a local woman, Mrs Babcock Cleaver, who lent the dog to civil defence units during the Second World War. Jet was born locally at Garth Drive, and was reputedly the first dog to be used in the war for such purposes and proved invaluable, helping to rescue buried people from bomb sites, particularly in the V1 'Doodlebug' raids of 1944 to 1945. He took his part in the Victory Parade in London in June 1946 with the civil defence units. In August 1947 he was called out of retirement to help in the William Pit mining disaster in Whitehaven, when he led rescuers to the victims and gave warnings of impending roof falls, which certainly saved the lives of the rescuers. He was often taken for walks in Calderstones Park, and died aged seven at home in 1948, but not before he had been awarded the Dickin Medal, the animal equivalent of the Victoria Cross. He was buried in the park on 22 October 1949. The memorial, by a Hoylake artist, is inscribed 'Jet belonged to mankind and never failed'.

A STONE COMMEMORATING ENGLAND'S POPULAR OUTLAW

Robin Hood's Stone, Booker Avenue, Allerton

Access

At the junction of Booker Avenue and Archerfield Road.

This upright slab of red sandstone is located behind railings in a small enclosure. It is almost 8ft tall, and is marked with deeply cut vertical man-made grooves facing southwards. The base of the stone, originally below ground and only now half visible, shows a cup-and-ring carving and several cup markings.

The stone was moved to its present location in August 1928 from its previous site in a field 198ft away called Stone Hey, which was being used for housing development. The field had at one time been owned by a Joseph Booker and it is said that it had been used for archery butts during Tudor times. A similarly carved stone was found at Haskayne in 1920. A metal plaque on the site indicates the direction of the previous location.

LIVERPOOL'S OLDEST BUILDING

Stanlawe Grange, Aigburth

Access

On the northern side of Aigburth Hall Road.

This building, now a private house, is sometimes claimed to be the city's oldest building. Built of sandstone, the oldest parts are believed to date from the thirteenth century, when land in the area was owned by the monks of Stanlawe Abbey, located in north Cheshire. The building started its life as part of a farm or 'grange' run by the monks of the abbey, and is sometimes referred to today as the 'Monks Granary'.

After the Dissolution of the Monasteries the land was leased to Lawrence Ireland for £4 per annum (see also page 90) and part of the estate awarded to the Savoy Hospital in London. By 1550 it was in the hands of the Tarleton family through marriage. The Tarletons were Catholics and it is claimed that the buildings were used to allow Mass to be celebrated, and their layout would have permitted this to take place in some degree of seclusion. In one of the old walls were carved inscriptions which may have represented the gravestone of two priests, buried here during the period when they were denied proper burials within cemeteries.

The Grange has been much altered over the years and both the farmhouse and other outbuildings have disappeared. The walls of the remaining building are over 2ft thick in places, cemented with red clay, and the original thatched roof has been replaced. The original oak beams also remain, held together by wooden pegs rather than nails.

REMINDERS OF THE BEATLES' EARLY DAYS

20 Forthlin Road, Mendips and Strawberry Fields Gates

No. 20 Forthlin Road is a terraced house on a 1950s council estate. Between 1955 and 1964 it was the home of the McCartney family. Many of the Beatles' earliest songs were composed and rehearsed here, and the group The Scaffold was also formed here.

The house was bought by the National Trust in the 1990s and has been carefully restored to its original condition. Inside, there are photographs and memorabilia, which together with an audio tour help to bring alive the music and memories of the people 'who were there'.

Access

Forthlin Road is off the western side of Mather Avenue (B5180). Mendips is on the eastern side of Menlove Avenue (A562), while the Strawberry Fields Gates are on the southern side of Beaconsfield Road, close to Menlove Avenue.

Mendips on Menlove Avenue, was the childhood home of John Lennon, where he lived with his Aunt Mimi and Uncle George. Lennon is reported to have said 'I lived in the suburbs in a nice semi-detached house with a small garden. Doctors and lawyers and that ilk living around.' Lennon composed early songs in his bedroom and on the front porch. The house was bought by Yoko Ono in 2002 and donated to the National Trust. After restoration it opened to the public in March 2003.

Mendips backed onto the Salvation Army hostel known as Strawberry Fields. As a boy, Lennon would play in the thickly wooded grounds, and the place became immortalised when the group released the single 'Strawberry Fields Forever' in 1967.

The home survived threat of closure in 1984, but the grounds have now been used for housing development. The famous gates have long been a stopping point for photographs on Beatle-city tours, bringing fans from all over the world. The gates have to be repainted periodically as fans like to leave their signatures on them. They were stolen in 2000, but were quickly recovered by police from a local scrapyard. The home finally closed in June 2005.

Neither Forthlin Avenue or Mendips can be visited without buying a ticket for the pre-booked tours, which start several times daily between June and September from Speke Hall or the Albert Dock.

The Penny Lane of the other famous song is located about half a mile further towards the city centre, along the A562, where Smithdown Road meets Penny Lane and Church Road. The shelter on the traffic island is now Sgt Pepper's Bistro. The local street signs are placed very high above the ground to prevent theft from over-enthusiastic fans.

LIVERPOOL'S HYDE PARK

The Palm House, Sefton Park

Access

Enter the park from Mossley Hill Drive, close to its junction with Ibbotson's Lane.

Sefton Park is the city's largest park, covering some 269 acres. The land was acquired by the Liverpool Corporation from the Earl of Sefton in 1867 and laid out to a design by local architects Lewis Hornblower and Edouard Andre, who won a competition that year. It was opened by the Duke of Connaught in 1872.

The Palm House was completed in 1896 and was a gift to the city by Henry Yates Thompson. It was designed by the Edinburgh firm of Mackenzie and Moncur. The building was over 70ft high, had 4,000 panes of glass and 12,000 metal parts. Its total cost was £12,000. Inside was a collection of exotic plants together with nine marble statues, including the *Whispering Angel* by Sir Benjamin Edward Spence, dating from 1850. Outside there were eight further statues, four in bronze and four in marble, of famous explorers and naturalists, including the Swedish botanist Carl Linnaeus. A cast-iron curved spiral staircase and catwalk were included.

During the Second World War the Palm House was camouflaged to prevent the glass reflecting moonlight and assisting German bombers. However, a bomb that fell nearby shattered all the glass, and it was not replaced until 1950.

The financial troubles of the local authority led to a period of decline for the Palm House as maintenance was cut back and vandalism took its toll. During the late 1980s the building was closed and all the glass removed. By 1992 public disquiet about the state of the Palm House led to a petition and a 'Save the Palm House' campaign. Subsequently a preservation trust was established and, together with the city council, money was raised from the Heritage Lottery Fund and other bodies. Work started in February 2000 when the building was dismantled piece by piece. The rebuilding was completed at a cost of £3 million in September 2001. The Palm House now looks magnificent. It has been adapted to be able to hold small-scale events. Unfortunately, to minimise future vandalism it has been necessary to build a large security fence around the building.

Sefton Park, or 'Sevvy' as it is sometimes called, should be a fine asset to the city. However, at the time of writing it was still suffering the effects of vandalism and underinvestment, and was crying out for a comprehensive restoration scheme. The old Pirate Ship has long since gone as has the statue of Peter Pan, by George Frampton, dating from 1928, which was in the middle of the lake. Only the base of Sir Alfred Gilbert's Eros Fountain remains. The top is currently being restored and copied, hopefully to be returned to its rightful place at some time in the future.

Commended for Bringing a Water Supply to Liverpool

Access

At the junction
of Gateacre Brow
(B5171) and
Grange Lane.

Wilson Memorial Fountain, Gateacre

This fountain, often called Gateacre Gazebo, commemorates John Hays Wilson of Lee Hall, Gateacre, who was chairman of the Liverpool Corporation Water Committee at the time the Lake Vyrnwy scheme of reservoirs was being pursued in the nineteenth century. He died in 1881, having caught a chill at a racing meeting held in the grounds of his home. The memorial was built by the people of Gateacre on land given by Sir Andrew Barclay Walker. The statue beneath the gazebo canopy has been missing for some time.

Close by, on Grange Road, are Soarer Cottages, built as 'model houses' in 1896 by William Hall Walker for the married grooms of his stables, to commemorate his Grand National victory.

A FLORAL TRIBUTE TO A MAN'S ASSOCIATION WITH AN ESTATE

Cuckoo Clock, Woolton Woods

This elegant floral clock was constructed in 1927 and was the gift of Miss Helen Gaskell, her mother and brother, in memory of another brother, Lieutenant Colonel James Bellhouse Gaskell, who had been brought up on the Woolton Hall estate.

The clock itself was made by James Ritchie & Sons of Edinburgh, and had some 18,670 plants. It was first set in motion at 3.30 p.m. on 29 July 1927. The minute hand was some 8½ft long and the hour hand 5ft long. A cuckoo call sounded at certain intervals, provided by a miniature organ pipe mechanism complete with bellows.

The clock was placed within the Walled Garden, a delightful spot which, when opened in 1921, was described as the 'finest Old English garden in the city'. It was designed by Harry Corlett, the estate's superintendent, and originally featured a sub-tropical plant house (below), a fountain and a bell at the upper end of the garden that tolled at the park's closing time.

Access

Within the Walled Garden at Woolton Woods, take a right turn from the School Lane entrance to the park.

The floral clock was neglected and its mechanism did not work for many years. The mechanism was restored in 2001 and a competition was organised the following year for local children to design the planting scheme for the clock face. The restored fountain and cuckoo clock won the Anne Farmer Trophy in the North West in Bloom competition in 2002 for the best special feature in a public garden.

In the adjoining Camp Hill Woods can be seen a mound reputed to be the site of an Iron Age hill fort.

LIVERPOOL'S OLDEST CINEMA

Woolton Cinema

Access

On Mason
Street, between
Church Road
and Woolton
Street.

This independently owned 255-seat cinema, which first opened on 26 December 1927, is the oldest surviving cinema in the city. Its original name, Woolton Picture House, is still visible above the entrance canopy. The architect was Lionel Pritchard.

Owing to the limitations of the site available, the cinema's auditorium had to be set at a considerable angle to the road frontage, and is only connected to the foyer on the far right-hand side. Originally the cinema had 800 seats, but with the introduction of the 'talkies' in about 1930 the number was reduced to 650 as the screen was moved forward to allow for the installation of sound speakers.

In the heyday of the cinema the Woolton was a typical 'family house', showing films after they had been released on the main cinema circuits. A serious fire on 22 September 1958 almost completely gutted the building, but it was rebuilt and modernised and an air conditioning system was installed. The seating capacity was further reduced to 612.

The building is now the only single-screen cinema in Liverpool, and until early 2004 it was one of the few such venues that continued to allow smoking on the premises. Unlike modern multiplex cinemas it still interrupts films with an ice cream intermission. Its small size, difficult-to-redevelop site and enterprising independent management have no doubt contributed to its continued viability.

The Woolton backs onto the village hall, which was the venue where the Beatles played their first gig. In those days the Picture House was commonly called the 'Bug House', similar to the 'flea pit' descriptions given to the many small and poorly furnished cinemas that were disappearing rapidly at the time. Today the cinema is well furnished and comfortable following a further modernisation in 1984 when the seating capacity was reduced to the present number.

THE OLDEST ELEMENTARY SCHOOL IN LANCASHIRE

Much Woolton Old School

Access

On the southern
side of School
Lane.

This stone building bears a foundation stone dated 1610, although there is some doubt about the true age of the building, as the final '0' on the stone is believed to have been added before 1930 by the then rector of Woolton, Archdeacon Howson. Some believe it was a Pre-Reformation chapel, others that it could date from 1641.

It is said to be the oldest elementary school in Lancashire, but was never a 'grammar' school. It ceased to be a school in 1848, and at various times since it has served as a cottage, a cowshed and as a store shed for Liverpool Corporation Parks Department.

For many years it was unused and derelict, but has now been returned to educational use and houses a pre-school day nursery. It is a Grade II listed building.

DINGLE'S ANCIENT CHAPEL

Ancient Chapel of Toxteth

Access

At the corner of Park Road and Ullet Road.

This is one of the oldest non-conformist chapels in the UK and is claimed to be the oldest original church in Liverpool. The congregation was founded in 1611 and the chapel itself was completed in November 1618, when Richard Mather began his ministry. The building was partly rebuilt in 1774 when three galleries and box pews were provided. William Latham's sketch from 1823 gives an idea of the original appearance of the building. A porch was added in 1841 and one of the bells dates from 1751. A memorial tablet was erected on the building in 1918. The adjoining meeting room was built in 1934.

Two other interesting religious buildings are to be found nearby at the junction of Princes Road and Upper Parliament Street in Toxteth. One is the Greek Orthodox Church, built in 1870, which has four domes on its roof. The other is the Princes Road Synagogue, built in 1874, which has a spectacular interior and is a Grade II* listed building. It has been described as Europe's finest example of Moorish Revival synagogue architecture.

A Remnant of the 'Docker's Umbrella'

Liverpool Overhead Railway Tunnel

Access

On the eastern side of Sefton Street, near the junction with Ellerman Road and the Riverside Business Park.

The Liverpool Overhead Railway ran, for the most part, on an elevated metal structure along the whole length of the city's dock system. It opened in January 1893 and ran from Seaforth and Litherland at the north end, where it connected with the main line system, via the Pier Head to Herculaneum Dock at the south end. It operated a frequent service with electric traction and was an early user of colour light signalling throughout. There were initially sixteen stations on the line.

Because of its elevated structure, which ran above the lines of the Dock Board's own internal railway system, it provided some shelter for dock workers when moving between docks and became known as the 'Docker's Umbrella'. In December 1896 an extension was opened which took the railway via this tunnel to the suburb of Dingle. The viaduct that took the line to the tunnel mouth was some 250yds long, and was the longest stretch on the railway.

The railway was not nationalised in 1948. It closed on 30 December 1956, as the costs of repairing the overhead structure of the whole line were considered prohibitive. The railway had been completely demolished by 1959, and now little trace remains, one exception being the entrance to the Dingle Tunnel.

See also the remains of the adjoining Herculaneum Dock where the special compartments built into the dock wall were necessary because of the petroleum products handled.

A REMINDER OF LIVERPOOL'S GARDEN FESTIVAL

Exit Barriers, Festival Park

Acess

On the western side of Riverside Drive.

In the early 1980s the government set up a number of initiatives to bring about the regeneration of many of Britain's cities. Enterprise Zones were created, and both London and the Liverpool Docks Development Corporations were established. Another initiative, set up by Environment Secretary Michael Heseltine, was to hold continental-style garden festivals on large unreclaimed sites as a means of bringing about their development.

Liverpool was the site of the first festival, using a large derelict site between the southern Docks and Garston known locally as the Cast Iron Shore. The organ-

isation of the festival was left to the Merseyside Development Corporation, which Heseltine fervently encouraged with his still legendary weekly visits to the city, between which he expected definite progress to have been made. The festival was held on a 125-acre site between May and October 1984, and was considered a success, attracting over 3 million visitors from home and abroad.

After the festival closed part of the site was handed over to developers for housing and commercial uses, but the seaward side had always been intended

for public use. Disagreements between the various authorities meant that this aspiration never came to pass. A smaller garden festival was held in 1985, and from then until the late 1990s commercial operators ran a Festival Park around the central Arena building. This has not operated for a number of years and the remaining parts of the site are now near derelict, although in 2004 it was announced by the city council, now the landlord of the site, that a new operator was to take over shortly and bring the site back to life.

The exit gates shown were not positioned here for the original festival, but would have been elsewhere on the site. They were moved here when Riverside Drive was built after 1985.

One or two remnants of the garden festival can still be seen in the area. A gazebo stands in Royden Park in Wirral and until recently the Yellow Submarine was located in Chavasse Park. This was removed in 2004 to allow development work to progress, but may reappear on another site in the future. A scale model of the Garden Festival layout, produced for the Merseyside Development Corporation, is in the Museum of Liverpool Life.

AN AIRPORT TERMINAL USED AS A HOTEL

Former Liverpool Airport Terminal

This hotel, tastefully extended and modernised, is the original terminal building for Liverpool Airport. The airport had opened in July 1933 under the auspices of Liverpool Corporation. Work on the terminal building, originally known as the Station Building, started in 1936. The building was a concave structure, with a control tower in the centre. The accommodation provided was spacious, as Liverpool was then the major airport in north-west England. The design of the Art Deco building and its adjacent hangars (both still standing) reflected the aviation theme down to the smallest detail; even the rainwater guttering had outlines of aircraft on it (see overleaf). The control tower was completed in June 1937 and the rest of the terminal in early 1939, just prior to the start of the Second World War.

Access

Now the Liverpool Marriott South Hotel, located about 5 miles from the city centre on Speke Road (A561) opposite the retail park. It is possible to walk round all sides of the building.

In the 1950s Liverpool Airport lost its pre-eminence in the region to nearby Manchester, and traffic began to decline. A new runway was built in 1966 near Speke Hall as the existing airfield was unable to cope with jet aircraft. A new and smaller terminal was opened in 1986, at which time the old terminal was closed. The building remained unused until developed as the luxury four-star Liverpool Marriott South Hotel by Neptune Developments and Whitbread, aided by the Speke Garston Development Company and the EEC. It opened on 29 June 2001.

In front of the building is a mock-up of a DH89 Dragon Rapide aircraft, built by enthusiast Mike Davey and friends and installed in September 2001. This twin piston-engined aircraft type, carrying only a few passengers, would have provided many services from the airport in the 1930s. On the other side of the terminal, on the former aircraft apron, is the Jetstream 41, a more modern aircraft donated by BAe Systems and restored in 2003 by members of Wirral Aviation Society. It is used for educational purposes, and there are regular open days.

2

CURIOSITIES OF KNOWSLEY

NAMED AFTER THE LANDOWNER'S ADDRESS

The Brick Wall Inn, Tarbock

Access

On the south side of Netherley Road (B5178), close to the junction with Greensbridge Lane.

The original pub to bear this name was built using handmade bricks and was a plain square building, probably built in the late seventeenth century, combining public house and farmstead. In 1614 Richard Molyneaux had acquired the manor of Tarbock. At the time he lived in Sefton Hall, located off Brickwall Lane in Sefton, and it is likely that the pub would have been built by him and named after his address.

In the 1830s three lodges of the Oddfellows were established in the Prescot area and one of them, the Farmers Rest Lodge, met in the Brick Wall Inn. To mark their foundation day each July they would march to Halewood via Greensbridge Road.

In the years up to 1880 beer for the pub was brewed by Fleetwood's across the road at premises now known as the Brewery House and Brewery Farm. Fleetwood's was bought by the Burtonwood Brewery Company in 1925, which improved the building. The current building dates from 1940 when it replaced the original structure.

A MEDIEVAL VILLAGE CROSS

Cronton Cross

Access

At the junction of Hall Lane and Smithy Road, at the northern end of the village.

The precise age of this medieval sandstone cross shaft is not known, although local parish records show that it was repaired in 1734. It had lost its cross head by 1906. It was originally situated opposite Cronton Hall at the meeting of roads now thought to be at Cronton Park Avenue, and was used as a resting point for funeral processions making their way to Farnworth church.

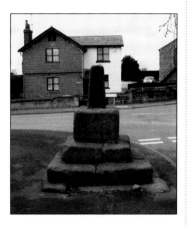

See also the Cronton village stocks at the junction of Smithy Lane and Cronton Road (A5080). Often located opposite the local pub, in this case the Unicorn Inn, they were introduced as punishments for minor offences such as drunkenness from about 1350. Another medieval cross can be found at Roby, further along the A5080, at the junction of Roby Road and Station Road. It was previously located nearby at the junction of Roby Road and Carr Lane.

BUILT TO COMMEMORATE QUEEN VICTORIA'S JUBILEE

Huyton Cross

Access

Located on Huyton village green, at the junction of Stanley Road and Blue Bell Lane.

This cross was built in 1897 in commemoration of Queen Victoria's Diamond Jubilee. It is made of sandstone, and apart from some graffiti, is reasonably complete. The cross comprises a slender shaft which has a niche at its top containing the figure of St Michael, after whom the local church is named.

No medieval cross ever stood on this site, but an earlier cross had been erected in 1819 to a design by Thomas Rickman. It was erected at the instigation of the Revd Ellis Ashton of St Michael's Church, who wished to see the village green used for a purpose other than cock fighting and bull baiting. It is reported that he had appealed to his congregation to have the sports banned, and on several occasions had remonstrated with those indulging in the sports until they had left the village green.

BUILT TO RESEMBLE AN ANCIENT CHAPEL

The Folly, Prescot

Access

Just inside the gates to the cemetery at the east end of Wood Lane, where it meets the footpath leading from Vicarage Place.

This short section of the Prescot Vicarage garden wall was built in the eighteenth century to look like an Anglo-Saxon ruin. It runs along the old medieval town boundary of Prescot, and is of later construction than the rest of the late seventeenth-century sandstone wall into which it has been built. It is sometimes called the 'gate feature'. It is claimed that there is some evidence of an ancient chapel on the site of the vicarage garden, and this small folly was built to look like the remains of it.

THE NARROWEST NAMED STREET IN THE COUNTRY

Stone Street, Prescot

Access

On the north side of the main shopping street of Prescot, Eccleston Street.

This narrow and steep cobbled street is claimed to be one of the narrowest, if not the narrowest, named street in Britain. It is on average only 2ft 6in wide, and at the lowest point narrows to a width of only 2ft where a drain-pipe of an adjoining building is sited. It leads northwards towards High Street and sees little use. It has changed very little from its origins in the seventeenth century.

GEORGIAN PRESCOT

Vicarage Place, Prescot

Access

In the centre of Prescot, between the parish church and the Deane's House pub.

The town of Prescot is one of the earliest settlements in Merseyside, and much of the town centre is a Conservation Area. Vicarage Place is an attractive street of

Georgian and neo-Georgian properties. Nos 4 and 6 were restored by the local authority in 1977. No. 8 is a completely new building behind a neo-Georgian frontage, currently used as retirement flats. Above the door is the coat of arms of the town of Prescot, based on that from King's College Cambridge, and which was originally sited on the old Town Hall, built in 1755 on Market Place, and demolished in 1965.

A STONE PROVIDED TO TEST LITERACY

Alphabet Stone, Prescot

Access

On the western side of Market Place.

The small area of tarmac in the paved area between Market Place and Prescot Parish Church is the site of the so-called Alphabet Stone. This stone was a door lintel above a lock-up that formed part of the old Prescot Town Hall, built in 1755, which stood on this site until 1965 when it was demolished amid local outcry.

The stone contains all the letters of the alphabet except the letter 'J', which was not used at the time. The letters are arranged in three columns and appear on their side. It is believed that the stone was used to test literacy.

In recent years the stone became increasingly weather-beaten and the letters have worn away considerably. To prevent further damage, the stone was removed from the site a few years ago. Some restoration work has been carried out on it and it is currently in store at Prescot Museum. However, the effects of the deterioration are such that it is unlikely to be displayed outside again, and its future awaits a decision by the local authority.

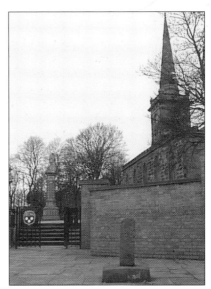

A REMINDER OF A PRIME MINISTER AND THE YOUNGEST EVER CABINET MEMBER

Pipe & Gannex pub, Knowsley

Access

On the northern side of Sugar Lane, off the B5202.

This 1960s public house, with its distinctive sign board, commemorates the one time Labour Prime Minister, Harold Wilson, who was MP for the Huyton constituency from 1950 until 1983. Wilson was rarely seen in public without his pipe, and both it and the Gannex raincoat were synonymous with him. The Gannex was made in his home town of Huddersfield.

Born in 1916, Wilson started his career as an academic, teaching economics, before becoming Director of Economics and Statistics at the Ministry of Fuel and Power in 1943. He entered parliament in 1945, and soon after became successively the Secretary for Overseas Trade and the President of the Board of Trade, at the age of twenty-nine, the youngest cabinet member since William Pitt the Younger. In 1963 he became leader of the Labour Party on the death of Hugh Gaitskill, serving as Prime Minister from 1964 to 1970, and again between 1974 and 1976, when he surprised everyone by resigning. He was made Lord Wilson of Rievaulx in 1983 and died in 1995 after suffering from cancer and Alzheimer's Disease.

Knowsley village itself is worth closer examination. It comprises an estate village of *cottage ornées* of similar design built at various periods in the nineteenth century by the Earl of Derby for his staff.

A STONE PROVIDED TO AID MOURNERS

Weeping Stone, Kirkby

It is not known precisely how old this sandstone pillar is, but it is thought to have been an ancient cross known as Part Brow Cross, which once stood near Park Brow, a short distance to the south-east of the present site, at what is now the junction of Bullers Road and Wellfield Avenue. Maps of 1769 and 1849 show its location as a field known as Cross Croft. Part is an Anglo-Saxon term for pear.

The cross was a typical 'weeping cross', in this case being the place where mourners carrying coffins to the Catholic burial grounds at St Swithins at Gilmoss would have set down their burdens and rested.

Between 1881 and 1890 the cross suffered damage when its arms were broken off.

The Earl of Sefton, William Philip Molyneaux, arranged for the cross to be put back on its previous site, in a square enclosure at Three Lanes End. At the same time it was cleaned and restored, and its broken shaft was re-shaped into the current pyramid-like obelisk, which is some 6ft in height.

The obelisk was affected by construction of Kirkby New Town in the 1950s when it was discovered again damaged and defaced. It was placed in its present position during the further development of Kirkby New Town in 1961.

Access

Located in the small park that lies between Old Hall Lane and Kirkby Row, just off the A506.

See also, nearby, in the churchyard of St Chad's, Kirkby or St Chad's Cross. This was erected between 1875 and 1876 when the 4th Earl of Sefton built the present church, the third such building. The cross marks the site of the previous building. It was vandalised in the early 1990s and the original cross head has been removed for safe keeping.

A Source of Fresh Food in the Eighteenth Century

Pigeon House, Kirkby

Access

At the junction
of Ingoe Lane
and Whitefield
Drive, opposite
the appropriately
named Fantail
public house.

This pigeon house was built in 1703 at the same time as the adjoining Whitefield House. At the time only the lord of the manor would have been allowed to keep pigeons, and they formed an easy source of fresh and tasty meat during the winter, as they bred several times a year. The building may also have been used as a dovecote and there was a small pigsty on its lowest level.

3

CURIOSITIES OF SEFTON

THE GRAVE OF A GREAT RACEHORSE

Red Rum's grave and statue, Aintree racecourse

Access

Located on the far side of the winning post at Aintree. The grave is not normally accessible at close hand, although tours of Aintree are available on a pre-booked basis.

This well-kept little grave and enclosure celebrates one of the world's greatest steeple-chaser racehorses who lived from 1965 to 1995, winning the Grand National in 1973, 1974 and 1977, and being runner-up in 1975 and 1976.

Owned by Mr N.H. Le Mare, Red Rum was trained by Southport-based Donald 'Ginger' McCain. Close to the winners' enclosure is a life-sized statue of the horse by Philip Blackler, commissioned by Seagram Distillers and unveiled by the Princess Royal on Grand National Day on 9 April 1988.

BUILT TO COMMEMORATE THE BATTLE OF WATERLOO

Potter's Barn, Waterloo, Crosby

Access

At the junction of Crosby Road South (A565) and Cambridge Road.

This curious building is located at the gateway to the small park that also bears the Potter's Barn name. It was built in 1841 by William Potter, owner of the merchants Taylor Potter & Company, traders with China. He intended to build himself a new house here to replace his previous house in Everton. The entrance gateway and coach house, which bear his initials and the date 1841, were built first. Unfortunately his business then failed and he was unable to complete the project.

The property then passed to a Mr Bibby and it became known as Bibby's Land, and later still was used as a cornfield. It eventually came into the ownership of the local authority. For a time nothing was done with the property and local press reports from 1903 tell of council unease in spending £40 to repair the buildings from the dilapidated state into which they had fallen. In 1908 the site was opened as a public park.

For many years Potter's Barn was said to resemble farms at La Haye Saint or Hougemont in present-day Belgium, on or near the site of the famous battlefield of 1815, but recently doubts have been cast on this, and a location at Mont St Jean has been suggested as an alternative.

The areas once called Crosby Seabank and Downlitherland were merged and called Waterloo after the battle, along with the large hotel in the area, the Royal Hotel, which has now reverted to its original name. Streets in the area are named after Wellington and Blucher, the victorious allied generals.

Potter's Barn has a rather neglected look to it today. A Friends of Potters Barn group was active for a number of years and campaigned for restoration. Currently, the local authority is understood to be looking at bringing it back into use as accommodation for its park ranger service.

Another of Crosby's small parks contains the Boulder Stone, a 20-ton erratic block of gypsum carried down to Crosby from Cumbria during the Ice Age. It was discovered in 1898 buried at a depth of 20ft on a site in Manor Road. Until 1926 it was positioned at the junction of Liverpool Road and Islington. It was then moved to Coronation Park on Coronation Road.

AN UNUSUAL WAR MEMORIAL

Five Lamps War Memorial, Crosby

This war memorial stands on a traffic island located on the bridge carrying the main road over the railway. It consists of a winged female figure holding a laurel wreath, standing on a small globe, itself positioned on a square pillar. Surrounding it are five ornamental lamps. The war memorial was built by the local authority between 1920 and 1921 to a design by Doyle Jones, and was unveiled and dedicated on 29 October 1921.

Ornamental lamps had been provided at this point for some years, as had a water trough. The location was an important stopping point on the tramway that used to run between Liverpool and Crosby, which opened in 1900. The designs of the lamps have varied over the years, and the current ones are not the originals. After the memorial was damaged some years ago the local authority carried out a full restoration, which was completed in October 1986.

Further to the north on the main road, in Crosby proper, is the well-known Merchant Taylor's School. Until the late 1960s this was the location of a 'curiosity', albeit not accessible to the public. Seated in the main hall of the girls' school, at a small desk and chair and dressed in the school uniform, was a doll known as Jane Harrison, named after the founder of the school, John Harrison. This doll first appeared in 1928 when it was provided at the suggestion of a pupil during a Creative Week held at the end of the summer term. The doll sat there for some forty years – 'the little girl who never grew up' – although her uniform changed with the seasons. Alas, during a fit of modernisation at the school both doll and desk were destroyed. Only the little chair remains, bereft of its former occupant.

A WINDMILL USED AS A HOUSE

Windmill, Crosby

Access

On the northern side of Moor Lane (A565).

There have been a number of windmills in Crosby since the thirteenth century. This one was built between 1813 and 1814 by local landowner William Joseph Blundell to replace an earlier one that had stood in Little Crosby. The present structure is six storeys high and some 69ft above sea level. In 1823 a new set of sails for the mill cost £17 2*s*, the miller paid an annual rent of £15 and his wage costs were £1 a week. The mill was powered successively by wind, steam, gas and finally electricity before finally ceasing production in 1972. It is now a private house.

See also, in nearby Lydiate, a similar windmill now converted as a private house on the northern side of Liverpool Road (B5407).

ONCE A SECRET BURIAL GROUND FOR CATHOLICS

The Harkirk Chapel, Little Crosby

Access

Not normally accessible to the public as it lies within the private grounds of the Crosby Hall Estate. It may, however, be seen when the annual Harkirk Mass is held, organised by the nearby St Mary's Roman Catholic Church in Little Crosby on a Sunday evening in July.

From the late sixteenth to the mid-eighteenth century Catholicism was a persecuted religion. Many who had remained true to the pre-Reformation Old Faith, often called recusants, were refused proper burials in their parish churchyards.

In December 1610 the authorities refused to allow the burial of a body of a local Catholic woman in the graveyard of St Helen's church, Sefton, and as a result her body was buried in a shallow grave by the roadside. The grave and body were subsequently disturbed and desecrated by grazing hogs. On hearing of this case local Catholic landowner William Blundell (1560–1638) of Crosby Hall resolved to make available a piece of land where Catholic burials could be carried out with some dignity. He chose a secluded spot on his estate thought to have been the site of an ancient Saxon chapel called the Harkirk. The woodland is now known as the Burying Ground Plantation.

Between 1611 and 1753 some 131 people were buried at the site, including 25 priests. The names were listed in a notebook kept by the Blundell family, which exists to this day. Often the burials took place at night, as Catholic practices were prohibited and the marking of graves with crosses was banned. In 1630 the local sheriff was ordered to destroy the illegal burial ground, so the fences and gravestones were torn down, but its use continued.

The current building was erected by Colonel Nicholas Blundell (1811–94) in 1889, using some of the stones found lying at the site. Three undamaged headstones were found and incorporated into the north wall near the door. A list of those buried at the site is to be found within the chapel.

AN ORNAMENTAL GATEWAY BUILT TO RESEMBLE A FEATURE FROM A PAINTING

Lion's Gate Lodge, Ince Blundell

This is one of several ornate entrance lodges to the Blundell family's Ince Blundell estate, which was surrounded by a wall built between 1760 and 1776. The gateway's design was taken from a detail in a painting in the family's art collection, 'The Marriage of Bacchus and Ariadne', painted by Sebastiano Ricci in about 1690.

Access

At the junction of Ince Lane (A565) and Park Wall Road.

THE MEETING PLACE OF THE 'MOCK CORPORATION OF SEPHTON'

St Helen's Church, Sefton

Access

At the junction of Bridges Lane and Lunt Road, just off the B5422. The church is only open for Sunday services, although open days take place on spring and summer Bank Holiday Mondays.

The church of St Helen's dates from 1170, and although not completed until the sixteenth century it features many items of interest, including an octagonal pulpit from 1635, an impressive Tudor rood screen and, some say, the most impressive collection of medieval and Tudor effigies, tombs and brasses in the country. Sometimes called the 'Cathedral of the Fields', it is the only Grade I listed building in the Metropolitan Borough of Sefton. The church's most famous rector was one Parson Nutter, who was once called The Golden Ass by Elizabeth I because of his wealth and ignorance.

At the rear of the church is a box pew with a brass plate inscribed with the words Corporation of Sephton. This Corporation existed in the eighteenth century and was a social group of Liverpool and Bootle gentlemen and merchants who gave mock titles to each other. Their titles included Butter Weigher, Ale Taster and Overseer of Bastard Children. They also had ministers with mock jurisdiction over little-known and undesirable parts of the British empire.

They were a lively crowd, and enjoyed their summertime leisure with liberal eating and drinking in the Punch Bowl Inn, toasting such matters such as the British successes in the Peninsular Wars. They also did charitable work, providing 100 pairs of flannel shorts for the troops.

The Mock Corporation attended St Helen's Church and sat in their own pew. Once a year they were joined at Morning Service by the boys of Blue Coat School from Liverpool. Their regalia was on show for many years in the Liverpool Museum, but most was lost in 1941 when the museum was damaged in the blitz.

THE OLDEST ECCLESIASTICAL BUILDING IN MERSEYSIDE

Ancient Chapel of Maghull

Access

The chapel lies at the rear of St Andrew's Church, located on Damfield Lane, off the A59.

This building dates from between 1280 and 1290 and is thought to be the oldest ecclesiastical building in Merseyside. The nave of the original building was pulled down in 1756, and in 1777 the chapel was totally rebuilt, using some of the old stones as foundations. Its function as Maghull's parish church ceased in 1878 when the adjoining St Andrew's Church was completed. All the chapel's later additions were removed in 1883, and only strong local opinion saved the demolition of the remainder at the same time.

The window in the lady chapel is particularly noteworthy. There is also a bell turret, traces of wall paintings, a mutilated piscine, a prism-shaped holy water font and a Georgian baptismal font. The lady chapel is sometimes called the Unsworth chapel, after the family who paid for the construction of the church. Some of the family are buried in the chapel.

Close to the chapel, in the graveyard, stands a marble memorial to Frank Hornby, one-time MP and the maker of popular toys of yesteryear such as Meccano, Dinky Toys and Hornby Dublo trains, who lived for a time in Maghull. An English Heritage blue plaque has been placed on his former house in Station Road.

PART OF OLD CATHOLIC LANCASHIRE

St Catherine's Chapel, Lydiate

Access

On the western side of Southport Road (A5147) to the north of Station Road.

This ruined chapel, sometimes mistakenly called Lydiate Abbey, was built for the private worship of the Irelands, lords of the manor of Lydiate from 1410 to 1673. Laurence Ireland (1410–86) is thought to have started the chapel in the late fifteenth century. He had married Catherine Blundell of Little Crosby and the chapel was dedicated to her and St Catherine of Alexandria. The initials LI and CI were carved in some of the stonework, but this is now lost.

The chapel was probably completed by their son John early in the sixteenth century, but was damaged at the time of the Dissolution of the Monasteries and its use ceased in about 1550. It was never a parish church, so it was one of the places in south-west Lancashire where Catholic worship could continue in secret. Jesuit priests were buried here for many years. It was roofless by the eighteenth century and suffered major deterioration in the nineteenth century. One recent writer has described it as 'a perfect specimen of a small Gothic ruin'.

The north wall of the chapel is windowless, possibly to avoid the cold northerly winds. Its construction has been claimed to be similar to Windleshaw Chantry at St Helens (see page 111), although its dimensions are larger. A carved figure of St Catherine and some alabaster reredos carvings, depicting her life, formerly in the chapel, are now in the nearby St Mary's Catholic Church after having spent some time in nearby Lydiate Hall.

The building is now a Grade II listed building and both it and the nearby Hall are part of a Conservation Area. Consolidation of the structure was undertaken between 1993 and 1994, and the building is now in the care of Lydiate Parish Church, supported by the North West Ecological Trust and the Friends of St Catherine's Chapel.

A RUINED MEDIEVAL HALL

Lydiate Hall, Lydiate

Access

Off Southport
Road (A5147)
immediately
adjacent to
Lydiate Hall Farm
Centre.

This ruined hall, partly hidden by trees, was built by the Ireland family who held the Lydiate Estate from 1410. The oldest parts of the building date from the first half of the sixteenth century. The hall was built by John Ireland II and originally comprised a quadrangular building, with three sides built of timber on a low sandstone cill, with the fourth side of stone construction. It is said that the Hall had certain similarities to Speke Hall and Rufford Old Hall.

The estate passed by marriage to Sir Charles Anderton in 1673 he did not occupy the hall but leased it to tenants. His son, however, did spend part of his retirement at Lydiate, and erected some of the adjoining farm buildings.

In 1760 the property passed to the Blundells of Ince Blundell. In 1778 a tenant demolished the old stone-built eastern wing, and in the nineteenth century the hall deteriorated so much so that by 1946 it was a complete ruin. The Leverhulme Estate bought it in 1951 and it is now a Grade II listed building.

In recent years the site has been tidied up and made accessible, thanks to the support of a number of private and public bodies. There are interesting information boards at the site that explain the hall's history and construction.

THE OLDEST PUBLIC HOUSE IN LANCASHIRE

Scotch Piper, Lydiate

Access

On the western side of Southport Road (A567) at the northern end of Lydiate.

The building dates from about 1550 and was probably built by Laurence Ireland II. It became a public house sometime around the middle of the seventeenth century and was first called the Royal Oak, as the visible parts of the cruck frame construction possibly gave rise to the belief that the pub was built around an oak tree. By 1823 it was called the Scotch Piper, a little later the Bag Pipes, and then the Old Lolly – perhaps after Laurence Ireland. Since 1891 it has been known as the Scotch Piper again.

The legend is that the name of the pub comes from an injured Highland piper who had taken part in the Jacobite rebellion of 1745, and who took refuge in the inn and later married the innkeeper's daughter. No hard evidence has come to light to substantiate this story, but the 700-strong pro-Hanoverian Blues raised by the Liverpool merchants at the time did capture a reconnaissance party of the Highlanders at Warrington and held them prisoner in Liverpool. They were later released and allowed to return home on their own accord. It is possible that one of these, at the end of his first day's walk from Liverpool, called at the inn and decided to go no further.

The pub was sold by the Lydiate Estate in 1922, and it was later bought by the Burtonwood Brewery in 1945. From 1961 to 1996 it was looked after by the popular Charles and Ada Rigby, and it remains a well-loved pub to this day.

A GIANT'S GRAVESTONE

Richard Formby Grave, St Luke's Church, Formby

Access

On St Luke's Church Road, about a mile south-west of Formby centre. The church is open on Sundays and Tuesdays between 2 and 4 p.m.

In the porch of the church is the large gravestone of Richard Formby, who died on 22 September 1407. He came from a wealthy background and his family home was Formby Hall. Standing some 7ft tall, he was ideal for the post of armour bearer to King Henry IV.

The gravestone was originally in York Minster, but was moved here in 1829 after a madman named Jonathan Martin set fire to the choir stalls. The resulting conflagration caused a roof beam to fall on the gravestone, which cracked and it exposed the bones in the grave. These were then measured and Richard Formby's height established.

The church itself only dates from the nineteenth century, but contains many interesting features, including a rose window featuring flowers local to the area, and a 23-sided font probably dating from the twelfth century and used in the first church that stood on this site.

The churchyard contains the grave of Percy French, the Irish poet and entertainer, the village stocks and the old village cross on which, so the story goes, in the eighteenth century a man sold his wife!

At the far side of the graveyard is the small carved Godstone, which it is suggested was either a pagan site or a means of converting the Vikings to Christianity.

THE HIGHEST BUILDING IN SOUTHPORT

The Round House, Hillside, Birkdale

Access

On the eastern side of Waterloo Road, overlooking the Royal Birkdale Golf Course.

This distinctive building, officially 61 Waterloo Road, is reputedly built on the highest point in Southport. It was constructed between 1924 and 1925 by Luke Highton (1850–1931), a builder who had spent some time in the United States. Aged seventy-four, his ambition was simply to build a house in the shape of a rotunda, and this he did at a cost of £8,000.

The building is constructed of red brick covered by roughcast. It was originally sited on a 12-acre plot, but much of this was sold off for subsequent development. On the roof was a 14ft diameter glass dome, intended as an observatory, from where there was an uninterrupted panorama of sea, sky, plains, local sandhills and the Cambrian and Cumbrian mountains.

At 5.30 a.m. on 29 June 1927, members of the British Astronomical Association, at Highton's invitation, used the roof and observatory to view a total solar eclipse.

Highton lived in the house until his death aged eighty-one. It has subsequently had a succession of owners and internal alterations, and in recent years has been well maintained. It was unoccupied for some years during the 1950s, during which time it lost its observatory. In 1999 it was listed as being of architectural and historic importance. On 21 January 1997 its interior was featured on the *House Style* television programme.

The building is so close to and visible from the famous Royal Birkdale golf course that it is often used by VIPs attending famous golfing tournaments that are held at the course. It is also, not surprisingly, used as a point of reference for golfers. One story goes that the famous American golfer, Lee Trevino, who won the Open here in 1971, once asked his caddy 'what's the line from here?' when playing the eighteenth hole. The man replied 'the Round House,' pointing out the house in the distance. Trevino was clearly unhappy at the response 'I know it's the Round House . . . but which window in the Round House do I aim at ?'

THE PLACE WHERE SOUTHPORT WAS BORN

Sutton Stone, Lord Street, Southport

Access

Adjacent to the roundabout at the southern end of Lord Street, at the junction with Duke Street.

Modern Southport is a comparatively recent development. A map produced in 1786 shows North Meols as the main settlement in the area; what is now Southport was a wilderness of sandhills. Nearby Churchtown was popular with bathers and visitors in the summer, but there was a 2-mile walk to the sea.

In 1792 William 'Duke' Sutton (1752–1840), the keeper of the Black Bull in Churchtown, built a bathing hut, occasionally used as a hostel, from driftwood gathered in the area. The hut, at a place called South Hawes, proved popular, and was repaired and improved after winter damage. The building was called Duke's Folly by the locals. In 1798 Sutton built a cottage next to the folly and arranged for a ship load of stone to be brought from Liverpool to build a hotel a short distance inland from the original site. The materials were unloaded at Southport which was the name given at a party thrown by Sutton and his friends the same year to celebrate the old Folly. The hotel was named the Original Hotel, later still the Royal Hotel and the Southport Hotel.

By 1854 the development of the resort had proceeded apace, and the hotel was effectively blocking the end of what had become Lord Street. It was then demolished and in 1860 a square memorial with carved plaques on its north-east and south-west faces was erected in its place by the local Improvement Commissioners. One of the plaques had previously been incorporated into the hotel. An ornamental light stood on top of the monument. In 1912 a road scheme caused the monument to be dismantled, and the plaques are now set into the boulevard wall at the side of the road.

Duke Sutton didn't profit greatly from founding the modern day Southport; he was obliged to give up his hotel in 1809 because of bankruptcy and ended his days in Lancaster debtors' prison.

A dresser, a violin, beer jugs from the hotel and an accounts ledger in Sutton's own hand can be seen at the Botanical Gardens Museum in Churchtown. A model of the hotel made by A.W. Kiddie in 1912 is also part of the exhibition.

THE MONTPELLIER OF ENGLAND

Lord Street, Southport

Access

In the centre of
Southport.

The wide boulevard of Lord Street has been renowned for its stylish shops for many generations, and was called the Montpellier of England in Victorian times. After Duke Sutton's early start in 1792 Bold Fleetwood Hesketh, then High Sheriff of Lancashire, took up residence in Meols Hall in Churchtown. Some of those who came to see him were impressed by the area and began to build homes along the road that ran from Churchtown to the beach. The road was first called Lords Street, after the two local landowning families – the Bolds and the Heskeths, later shortened to the present Lord Street.

Early developments included Wellington Parade (1817–18), Christ Church (1821) and the former Victoria Baths (1839). In 1825 an Act of Parliament was promoted by the local landowner, Peter Hesketh Fleetwood, who named Lord

Street, which stipulated that the street should not be less than 88yds wide. It also established Improvement Commissioners for the town to oversee its development.

The first railway arrived in 1848 and the Town Hall was opened in 1853. By 1867 the town had its own Borough Council. The Cambridge Hall and the Atkinson Library and Art Gallery, both buildings with great decorative ornamentation, followed in the 1870s. In 1871 one writer described Southport as 'a city of green lanes'.

The building on the left-hand side is the former Cheshire Lines Committee railway station. This opened in 1884, but closed in 1952, after which it served as a bus station for the Ribble Bus Company. More recently the rear train shed has been demolished and used as the site of a new supermarket, with the old station frontage being retained and restored.

ONE OF SOUTHPORT'S MOST VISITED BUT CONTROVERSIAL ATTRACTIONS

Red Rum Statue, Wayfarer's Arcade

Access

Located in Wayfarer's Arcade, which is on the western side of Lord Street.

This small bronze statue of the famous steeplechaser was sculpted by Lady Annette Yarrow and unveiled on 1 August 1979. Its cost of £7,500 was raised by public subscription. Not everyone likes it, and Red Rum's trainer 'Ginger' McCain described it as looking 'a bit plump and heavy' and 'thick-set and short' when it was first unveiled. Years later, when a proposal was being made to lend the statue to the National Horseracing Museum, he is said to have described it as looking 'more like a donkey' than his favourite Rummy. Despite this, every year thousands of people visit the statue and leave packets of mints and flowers by its hooves in affectionate memory.

THE SECOND LONGEST PIER IN BRITAIN

Southport Pier

Access

Via either the
Promenade or
Marine Drive.

This pier stretches for quite a distance over the Marine Lake, Princes Park and Marine Drive before it reaches Southport Beach. Even then, only at high tide is its outward end surrounded by water.

The company which built the pier was founded by Samuel Boothroyd in 1859. Built by Galloways of Manchester to a design by James Brunlees, a railway engineer from London, the 1,200yd-pier opened in August 1860. It was lengthened by 260yds in 1868 and a cable tramway was installed to transport visitors along it some years before San Francisco started its famous network. It was the longest pier in Britain until Southend pier opened in 1897. The sea was much closer to Southport in those days and pleasure boats operated to places like Anglesey, Blackpool and Llandudno until 1923.

In 1897 the pavilion at the seaward end was destroyed by fire and was replaced by a new one, which opened in 1902. George Formby and Gracie Fields both performed there. After a fire in 1933 the pier was bought by the local council and restored. There was another fire in 1959 when the pier was reduced in length, and in 1969 the pavilion was replaced by the present structure.

The pier is now a listed building and has again been restored with a striking glass structure at the far end. The pier railway was removed in the 1980s, and although tramtracks have been laid in the pier decking transport, when provided, is supplied by a 'road train'.

Southport is one of the few places in Britain where cars may be taken onto the beach.

THE SMALLEST PUBLIC HOUSE IN THE COUNTRY

Access

On the northern part of the Promenade, close to its junction with Leicester Street, overlooking the Marine Lake.

Lakeside Inn, Southport

Affectionately known as the 'Tardis', after the famous police-box in *Dr Who*, this friendly little pub is recognised as the smallest in Britain. To verify this a certificate signed by Norris McWhirter, editor of the *Guinness Book of Records*, is on display in this nautically themed pub.

The Lakeside Inn is officially lisenced for fifty people, but many attempts are made by visitors to see how many more can fit into the building. Some of its many regulars are said to be members of the Special Air Services (SAS) regiment from Hereford.

There is a Lakeside Inn in Kelseyville, California. Its proprietors have succeeded in making it a genuine reproduction of the Southport pub in many respects, with British beers, bar fittings and 'pub grub'. Although quite small, it does have a conference room.

WHERE OUR CHILDREN USED TO BE EDUCATED

Churchtown School

Access

On St Cuthbert's Road in the village centre, opposite the church.

What is now the attractive suburb of Churchtown has a long history. It was originally a fishing village and was once more important than its larger near neighbour. It is said that it is one of the most photographed villages in the Borough of Sefton, with many thatched cottages and the ancient parish church of St Cuthbert.

Education for the area was first provided by a grammar school built next to the churchyard, where both English and Latin were taught. The school was rebuilt by 1720 by the two local lords of the manor, Bold and Hesketh, assisted by an endowment left in 1684 for the purpose by the Revd James Starkey. That building was pulled down in 1826 and replaced by new schools for both boys and girls in the building photographed. In 1828 it is recorded that it catered for fifty-eight boys and seventy-eight girls.

This school was enlarged in 1837 to provide space for infants, but was replaced in 1859 by a new school built on a site to the north-west of the church further up St Cuthbert's Road. After serving for some fifty years, this building was demolished to be replaced between 1911 and 1913 by the current primary school. The 1826 school has been the local Conservative Club for some time. Plaques on its walls commemorate the 1826 building and its enlargement in 1837.

While in Churchtown, be sure to visit the nearby Botanical Gardens and its museum. The gardens were founded in 1874 by a company formed by the Mayor of Southport on land purchased from the Hesketh Estate. The museum opened in 1876 and featured local curiosities and other attractions. The botanical gardens company ran the gardens and museum on a commercial basis. It was declared bankrupt in 1932 and the land was bought by Southport Corporation in 1936 from a private developer. The museum reopened in 1939. Much of the collection is devoted to the area's local history, including the Southport Seaside Garden City exhibition.

A SEASIDE WARNING BELL

Marshside Fog Bell, Southport

Access

On the northern
side of
Marshside Road.

The suburbs of Marshside was once a hamlet situated next to a saltmarsh, reclaimed from the sea. The sea was formerly much closer to the settlement than it is today. The fog bell was first erected in 1876 with the aim of preventing a similar disaster to that which happened on 26 January 1869 when seven local fishermen lost their lives on the marshes while out 'shanking' (shrimping) during a fog. The names of all seven are listed on a plaque at the site.

The bell replaced a foghorn which for many years could be seen at the Botanical Gardens Museum in Churchtown. Following reclamation of the foreshore, the bell was removed to its present location in 1896. The bell is not used any more, but the area was restored in 1998, and the following year the feature had been vandalised.

4

CURIOSITIES
OF ST HELENS

BRITAIN'S FIRST PURPOSE-BUILT CANAL

New Double Locks, St Helens Canal

Access

About 5 minutes
on foot via the
canal towpath
northwards from
where the canal
crosses
Waterside or
Standish Street.

The St Helens or Sankey Canal, sometimes referred to locally as the 'Hotties', was authorised by Act of Parliament in 1755. Built at a cost of £200,000, it was designed by Henry Berry, who was the Port of Liverpool's second dock engineer. It was carrying coal by 1757, making it the first canal of the Industrial Revolution, predating the Bridgewater Canal, for which the claim is often made. (Strictly speaking, both canals should share the honours: the St Helens Canal carried goods first, while the Bridgewater was the first totally artificial canal, not being based around an existing watercourse like the St Helens Canal with the Sankey Brook).

The canal was built to supply coal to Liverpool's growing chemical industries, which subsequently spread back along the canal to establish themselves between Widnes and St Helens. The canal was a commercial success. It started to decline in the mid-nineteenth century and the upper part closed in 1931. However, the final traffic, of sugar to Earlestown, did not cease until 1959.

New Double Locks were first built in 1770 when a new branch on the canal was built to serve the growing industries of the Ravenhead area of the town. The locks were rebuilt in the 1850s after chemicals in the water rotted the mortar in the lock walls. The Ravenhead branch closed in 1898 and the original lock-keeper's cottage was demolished in the 1970s, reflecting, by then, the derelict state of the waterway.

Restoration of the locks began in 1986 when volunteers from the Sankey Canal Restoration Society cleared out debris. Full restoration was carried out in 1991 by the local authority using grant aid, with the Society using its connections within the canal restoration movement to get replacement lock gates from the Rochdale Canal Society.

Although other parts of the canal have been 'tidied up' as part of the Sankey Valley Country Park and some locks restored, reopening of the whole canal to navigation still appears to be some time off and New Double Locks now appear somewhat neglected.

In the background can be seen the Burgy Banks or Sand Lodges, areas of tipped waste material from the town's glass industry.

THE CENTRE OF THE WORLD'S GLASS INDUSTRY

Pilkington Head Office site

Access

Off Prescot Road (A58) about half a mile south-west of St Helens town centre.

The world-famous Pilkington glass company was first established in 1826 as the St Helens Crown Glass Company by William Pilkington and others. By the late 1830s control was in the hands of the Pilkington family, and the firm grew relentlessly through expansion and acquisition throughout the nineteenth and twentieth centuries. The peak of its achievement came in 1959, when it began mass production by the innovative float glass process.

This attractive head office campus was built between 1960 and 1964 when the firm needed a replacement for its previous head office on Grove Street, which had become too small. The development was designed by architect Maxwell Fry, of Fry, Dew and partners.

The central twelve-storey tower block is 159ft high and has blue-toned glass cladding. Inside are artist-designed glass murals. The conference room had what was claimed to be the largest glass table in the world, measuring over 40ft by 8ft. A total of 255,000 sq. ft of space was provided.

Adjacent is a smaller building designed for the firm's museum and lecture theatres. The whole development surrounds an ornamental lake, an extension of the old Ravenhead works reservoir, in the centre of which is a 28ft high fountain. At the northern end of the lake is the canteen building, which again has interior murals.

The whole complex cost some £5 million and was completed between 1963 and 1964. The Pilkington Glass Museum was opened in November 1964 by Sir Kenneth Clarke and the design won a Civic Trust award in 1966. At the time the complex was designed to cater for 1,600 staff, and it was thought that it would meet the firm's requirements for some fifty years.

More recently, the firm rationalised to meet increasing world competition, and the need for a large head office diminished. Parts of the site, known as Alexandra Park, are now let to other occupiers, and the Pilkington Glass Museum closed when many of the exhibits were transferred to the new World of Glass Museum. It nevertheless remains an impressive piece of 1960s architecture.

THE POOR MAN'S CATHEDRAL

Access

Located on the western side of North Road, at its junction with Crab Street, a few hundred yards north of the town centre.

St Mary's RC Church, Lowe House

This church is easily identifiable by virtue of its large green copper dome, which sits on a square tower. The origins of the church go back to 1742 when the local lord of the manor, John Eccleston, died. His widow decided that she would carry on the tradition of helping priests and local Catholic families, using her maiden name, Winefred Lowe, and she opened one of the rooms in her house so that Masses could be said. She then bought land on Crab Lane and built a church on it, although she died in 1793 before it was completed.

To cater for a growing congregation, a new building was planned from 1912. The then parish priest, Father Reginald Riley, had visited Belgium and wanted a Byzantine/Romanesque style of building, although the duomo (or cathedral) in Florence has also been suggested as the inspiration. The building was designed by C.P. Powell and opened in October 1929. The tower features a forty-seven-bell carillon and a chiming clock, donated by Pilkington Brothers in 1930, plays the melody of the Catholic hymn 'Salve Regina' on the hour.

In the grounds of St Mary's can be found a reproduction of the Hill of Calvary and a grotto.

At the nearby Landings roundabout, where North Road meets King Street and Baldwin Street, is the St Helens Mining Monument, celebrating the area's long connection with coal mining. This is a piece of modern sculpture in cast iron designed by Tom Dagnall; it was finished in 1996. It depicts members of the once thriving mining community: a pick-swinging miner, a young pitlad and a pitbrow lass. The three figures are positioned against a pillar of coal set on a piece of local Ravenhead stone. Landings was the name of a local junction between different underground roadways.

THIS MONUMENT HAS BEEN MOVED TWICE

Anderton Shearer Mining Monument

This sculpture was commissioned in the 1960s by Lord Robens, chairman of the National Coal Board, to celebrate the invention by James Anderton of the Anderton shearer and loading machine, which revolutionised modern deep-level coal mining and which was first used at the local Ravenhead Colliery in 1952.

The monument, designed by Arthur Fleishmann, was first erected in 1965 outside the Coal Board's North Western regional offices at Lowton. In 1989 it was moved to Eastwood Hall in Nottingham, and finally to its current location in December 1998 when the locally based Ravenhead Renaissance Partnership secured grant aid as part of a local regeneration initiative. The sculpture shows the head, hands and upper body of a miner emerging out of the blades of the cutting drum of the machine.

Access

In the middle of the Cannington roundabout, where the A58 meets the A569.

THE STATUE THAT KEEPS BEING MOVED

Queen Victoria, Victoria Square

In the Coronation year of 1901/2 the mayor, Colonel W.W. Pilkington, offered to donate a statue of the recently departed queen to the town. The borough council gratefully accepted the offer, and George Frampton, who had earlier designed a similar monument for Leeds Corporation, was commissioned to do the work.

The statue, a modified version of the Leeds design, was unveiled by Pilkington on 15 April 1905. In his speech on the occasion he referred to its location in the heart of Victoria Square, with its Town Hall, courts and Gamble Institute, as reflecting the ideals supported by the late queen, namely high standards of government and authority, learning, justice, art and science.

The statue was designed to face the Town Hall, but on the day before its unveiling it was re-sited to face Corporation Street. In 1910 Colonel Pilkington arranged for it again to face the Town Hall. In recent years it has been moved once more; this time to the western side of the square. Again, Victoria does not face the Town Hall.

THE OLDEST QUAKER MEETING HOUSE IN LANCASHIRE

Friends Meeting House, Church Street

This low stone-mullioned chapel is one of the most attractive buildings in St Helens, recently enhanced by a landscaping and floodlighting scheme. A sundial is positioned above the main entrance doorway.

Landowner George Shaw of Bickerstaff had become a Quaker after the founder of the Quaker movement, George Fox, had recruited many followers during his visits to the area in the middle of the seventeenth century. Shaw wanted to use a barn at Hardshaw, and by installing one Roger Taylor as a tenant he was able to register it as a chapel in 1658. Quakerism initially generated much opposition and the early years for the chapel were difficult times until the passing of the Act of Toleration in 1689.

In 1694 Shaw bequeathed the chapel and 23 acres of land to the Hardshaw Monthly Meeting. As a result, the chapel owned much of the surrounding land and was able to benefit financially from the growth of the town in the eighteenth and nineteenth centuries. The chapel was rebuilt in 1763. Shaw is commemorated in the adjoining street name.

Access

On the north side of Church Street, close to its junction with Shaw Street.

A MEMORIAL TO THE FOUNDERS OF BEECHAMS PILLS

Beecham Clock Tower, Westfield Street

Access

On the southern side of Westfield Street.

This distinctive ornamental clock tower stands at the corner of the former Beecham's head office, itself built on the site of the first Beecham factory in the town.

Thomas Beecham was born in Oxfordshire in 1820. In 1847 he moved to Wigan and was granted a medicinal licence. 'Dr Beecham' (as he then styled himself) moved to St Helens in 1858/9 and established a postal business in patent medicines. The business grew rapidly, especially in the 1880s, so much so that by 1890 some 9 million pills a day were being sold.

The clock tower was built in the Queen Anne style at a cost of £30,000 between 1885 and 1887 and was designed by the architect Hugh Krowlow. Each side of the tower is different, but it is largely symmetrical. A bust of the firm's founder is located in the arch keystone of the entrance below. The arch spandrels have figures bearing the words 'worth a guinea a box, largest sale in the world', used in early advertising of the firm's major product. In the 1950s the tower had 'The Home of Beecham's Pills' in large lettering on its main street elevation.

The tower contains a clock supplied by Potts of Leeds. Costing £1,000 at the time, it was designed so that its chimes sounded like Big Ben. The building was vacated by Smith Klein Beecham when the old factory was demolished in 1996, and is now used by St Helens College. There is a Beecham's Bar and Brewery on part of the ground floor.

THE OLDEST BUILDING IN ST HELENS

Windleshaw Chantry

Access

Adjoining the
St Helens
Borough
Cemetery, off
Hard Lane, or
alternatively via
Abbey Road.

Often mistakenly called Windleshaw Abbey, this building is thought to be the oldest building in St Helens. Built in 1435 by Sir Thomas Gerard of Bryn, it was a chantry chapel dedicated to St Thomas of Canterbury, where Masses could be said for the souls of his ancestors.

Built of local yellow sandstone, its Gothic-style tower is some 36ft high and 12ft square, with the building measuring 50ft long and 12ft wide. It has had a chequered history. Although it survived the Dissolution of the Monasteries under Henry VIII, in 1547 its closure was ordered under the Chantries Act and Sir Thomas Gerard, successor to the founder, was unable to gain exemption. The accession of the Catholic Mary to the throne in 1553 afforded some relief, and Masses continued to be celebrated there until about 1560. It remained in good condition until 1644, when it was partly demolished in the Civil War.

From the early eighteenth century the land around the chantry became a Catholic burial ground, many interments taking place at night in secret. Some sixty priests and one bishop are buried there. The burial ground was officially walled off in 1778 and extended in 1835.

Ownership of the chantry passed out of the Gerard family in the early twentieth century, but before that Dean Austin Powell of Birchley had persuaded Lord Gerard to donate land for a new school and church at nearby Denton's Green. The church opened in 1911 and is also dedicated to St Thomas of Canterbury. Its design is said to have been partly based on Windleshaw Chantry. The Chantry itself is in an attractive setting, and the tower has recently been restored, but, alas, continues to suffer from vandalism and litter. The stone cross in the churchyard dates from 1629.

THE HIGHEST POINT IN MERSEYSIDE

Billinge Beacon

Access

Via public footpaths which lead off the south side of Crank Road near Beacon Farm, about half a mile west of the junction with the B5206.

Billinge Beacon is located on the prominent landmark Billinge Hill, known locally as The Lump, at nearly 600ft in height the highest point in Merseyside and clearly visible from ships in the Mersey Estuary. It is said that on a clear day some sixteen English counties, Ireland, Scotland, the Welsh hills and the Pennines can be seen from this popular panoramic viewpoint.

The Beacon is a stone square structure that was constructed in 1788 as a summerhouse or folly by the Bankes family from the nearby Winstanley Hall. It has suffered from graffiti and vandalism over the years and its entrances have been sealed. In 1999 it was cleaned by the Groundwork organisation using moneys from a landfill tax credit scheme, but, as can be seen, some graffiti has returned.

The name comes from the fact that fires would have been lit on the hill top in times past to give warning of dangers and emergencies, such as the Spanish Armada in 1588. A fire lit in 1935 to celebrate the Silver Jubilee of George V damaged the original pyramid-shaped roof, which was then removed.

A local campaign was mounted in the 1970s when quarrying on the south side of the hill threatened the setting of the Beacon. The campaign secured the ultimate filling-in of the quarry when operations ceased, which has now occurred. In July 1988 another bonfire was lit on the hill to commemorate the defeat of the Armada 400 years ago.

The churchyard of St Aidan's, Billinge, contains the unusual tombstone of George Smith and his wife, dating from 1720. It is shaped like a coffin, with carvings of a serpent and a skull on the surface.

A WELSH CHAPEL IN ENGLAND

Welsh Chapel, Sutton Oaks

Access

At the junction of Sutton Road and Lancots Lane.

This little chapel, now a listed building, was built as a Wesleyan Methodist Chapel in 1845. Its side walls are constructed from cobbles made in moulds from copper slag, a by-product of the smelting and refining processes that took place at the many copper works that were established in the locality. Many local walls and some seven other churches in the area were also built using this material, donated in this case by the firm of Newton Keats & Company.

The site of the chapel was originally owned by Mr Blinkhorn, the manager of the London and Manchester Glass Company. The Methodists moved to a larger chapel nearby on Sutton Road in 1871, with the old chapel then being used as a Sunday school.

Many Welsh from North Wales and Anglesey had migrated to the area in the eighteenth and nineteenth centuries after the copper industry was first established at Ravenhead in the 1780s. It is said that church services in the Welsh language were held in private houses from about 1834. Subsequently larger accommodation was used at the Crone and Taylor factory in Lancots Lane opposite the current chapel. To get to services, churchgoers had to pass through a hole in the wall surrounding the factory, and for many years the Welsh church was known as the 'Hole in the Wall Church'.

The present building was acquired from the Methodists by the Welsh United Religious Church in September 1893, when it was extended slightly by the addition of a schoolroom and caretaker's house. Services were held in Welsh, with only the occasional event in English, although this position was reversed in the last ten or so years of the chapel's existence when it became difficult to obtain ministers to take the services. The chapel was always non-denominational and totally independent, although broadly non-conformist in nature.

Like many churches and chapels in recent decades, its congregation declined and attendances in single figures were the norm at regular services, although special events were well attended and there was generous support from the area's other churches. After being kept going for many years through the stalwart efforts of two redoubtable sisters, Bronwen and Gwladys Jones, regular services ceased in mid-2002 after Bronwen had died. The final special service was held in early December 2003 and the future of this interesting little building is currently uncertain.

THE CHURCH OF THE THREE SAINTS

Church of St Anne and Blessed Dominic, Sutton

Access

On Monastery Road, which is off Robins Lane.

This modern Catholic church contains the bodies of three individuals held in very high regard within Roman Catholicism. These are Ignatius Spencer, from whom the late Princess Diana is descended, the Blessed Dominic Barberi, a prospective saint, and Mother Elizabeth Prout, the foundress of the Sisters of the Cross and the Passion.

**The Servant of God
Fr Ignatius Spencer
Passionist
1799-1864**

Crusader of prayer for England and pioneer of ecumenical prayer, Fr Ignatius Spencer was born the Hon. George Spencer on 21st December 1799, the youngest son of the second Earl Spencer. Educated at Eton and Cambridge, he took orders in the Church of England but increasing doubts led him to become a Catholic. He was ordained priest in 1832. In 1846 he joined the Passionists (taking the name Fr Ignatius) and travelled all over England, Ireland and the continent of Europe, preaching and seeking prayers for England. He died on 1st October 1864 and is buried in the Passionist church at Sutton, St Helens. His cause of canonization was introduced in June 1992.

Blessed Dominic of the Mother of God,
Passionist

**The Servant of God
Elizabeth Prout**
(Mother Mary Joseph of Jesus C.P.)
Foundress of the
Sisters of the Cross and Passion
1820 - 1864

Elizabeth Prout was born in Shrewsbury, England, in 1820. Baptised in the Anglican Church, she became a Catholic in her early twenties. In 1851 she founded a religious community to care for the poor and abandoned, basing its rule and spirit on the teaching of St. Paul of the Cross, recognising that the Passion of Jesus is the great sign of God's love reaching out to those in pain. She died on 11th January, 1864 at Sutton, St. Helens, Merseyside, England.

The idea of a church on this site started in 1848 when the head of the Passionist order, General Anthony Testa, asked Dominic Barberi to find houses in England where Catholics could settle. Barberi subsequently acquired premises in London, Gloucester and Stone, and in January 1849 he sent Ignatius Spencer to see the Catholic bishop of Liverpool, George Hilary Brown. After refusing an offer to be domestic chaplain to the Blundell family near Crosby, Barberi sent Spencer and another priest to see John Smith, the contractor to the newly built St Helens Railway, who had offered to donate 12 acres of land and build a church, and shortly afterwards a monastery for the Passionist order.

The church was finished in 1851 and the monastery in 1855. After Barberi's death in 1849, Ignatius Spencer succeeded him as Superior of the Passionist Order. The original church was badly affected by mining subsidence and its tower was demolished in 1934. The church was demolished in 1973, and a new church was opened on 25 November 1973 by the Catholic archbishop of Liverpool, Archbishop Beck, the bodies of the three 'saints' being transferred in the process.

TRANSFERRED FROM HAYDOCK PARK

Randalls Archway, High Street, Newton le Willows

Access

Located on the
north side of
High Street,
close to its
junction with the
A572.

This archway was originally built by the Leigh family as one of the entrance lodges to Haydock Park in the 1780s, over half a mile north of its present site. The ram's head over the centre of the arch comes from the Legh (sometimes Leigh) family coat of arms and has become synonymous with Newton le Willows, now being part of the town crest.

The building was moved here in 1840 in order to serve as the centrepiece of Newton's market, re-established that year by the Leghs. It was known as the Market House and this section of High Street was known as Market Street. One wing of the archway was fitted out with stalls for traders, while the other was used for the sale of hardware, toys and so on.

The success of the market at Newton was not long-lived, as the nearby one at Earlestown soon re-established itself, and became permanent in 1870. The building then became part of the nursery garden business of John Randall & Sons, which operated on land to the rear, and the eastern wing was converted into a house for the owners. This use continued until the late 1980s when the land at the rear was sold for housing development, although the archway continued as a garden centre until the mid-1990s.

A proposal to demolish the archway in 1981 fortunately did not succeed. In 2001/2 work started on converting the archway into an Italian restaurant, which has involved a new building being added at the back. The restaurant finally opened as the Ariete in September 2004.

Nearby on the pavement are metal post holes where posts would be slotted each market day, so that the traders could secure their cattle and horses to prevent escape.

PUNISHMENT FOR WRONGDOERS OF THE PAST

Parish Stocks, Newton le Willows

Access

At the northern end of Church Street, in front of St Peter's Church.

It is not known how long these stocks have been located here, but it is thought that stocks have been used here since at least 1353. Responsibility for them fell to the churchwardens and sidesmen of the church who visited local hostelries on Sundays, which were not supposed to open until after the afternoon church service had finished. Anyone found disobeying this ruling would be likely to end up in the stocks. Dishonest traders and drunkards could expect the same punishment. The stocks were last used officially in 1859.

The adjoining church built in the 1890s has a square tower. The clock face on the northern side (away from the road) is not lit up at night. This was arranged at the behest of local printing company owner George McCorquodale who lived in The Willows, a large house formerly in what is now Willows Park, who did not wish the light to shine into his bedroom at night.

EARLESTOWN'S 'MILLY STONE'

Earlestown Cross, Market Place

This cross was first erected in 1818 in the yard of St Peter's Church at Newton le Willows to replace an earlier wooden cross bearing the arms of the local Leigh family. It was the gift of Lord Newton, whose family owned Lyme Park, near Disley in Cheshire.

The cross is constructed of bathstone and weighs 20 tons. Local legend states that the stone came from Lyme Park, and that it took a team of twenty horses seven days to bring the stone to Earlestown, breaking several bridges on the way. This story is now considered unlikely as bathstone is not found at Lyme Park. The cross was moved to its present site in June 1870. The obelisk became known as the Market Cross because the charter of the fair was read out from the steps on the opening of the May and Autumn fairs.

THE WORLD'S FIRST RAILWAY VILLAGE

Vulcan Village

Access

Located on Wargrave Road, which leads from Earlestown towards Winwick.

The village of Earlestown, located on the Liverpool and Manchester Railway roughly halfway between the two cities, became the first railway junction when the Warrington and Birmingham Railway was built. It was the ideal place for both a wagon and locomotive works to serve the new and rapidly expanding industry. The wagon works was established by Hardman Earle, after whom the village is named. The locomotive works, called the Vulcan Foundry, was founded in the 1820s by Charles Tayleur and by George Stephenson's son, Robert.

Between 1833 and 1841, to house the growing workforce, Vulcan Village was built. A school was completed in 1839. The terraced houses are arranged in rows forming a triangular shape, each being named after famous railway towns of the time. Originally there was a village green, but this was developed at a later date with a bath and washhouse and the Vulcan Inn.

The fortunes of the Vulcan Foundry rode high for many years, and locomotives were exported all over the world. In the 1950s, as steam traction began to be phased out on the railways, the factory produced the famous Deltic class of diesel locomotive, but in recent years it suffered a long and gradual decline. After being operated by English Electric Diesels, Ruston Diesels and finally Alstom, it finally closed in April 2003. Parts are now being redeveloped as light industrial units.

The village, however, has been retained. Although the local authority considered buying it in the 1970s for possible demolition, this did not happen. Between 1983 and 1990 it was sympathetically restored by the Maritime Housing Association at a cost of £3 million, the completed work being dedicated on 17 May 1990 by HRH the Princess Royal. The old school building has been converted into housing and there are now 120 units in the village.

Incorporated into two of the gable ends of the houses are the old works plaque from 1907 and some notices from 1835 that make it quite clear who was not welcome within the confines of the village.

THE SITE OF THE WORLD'S FIRST RAILWAY ACCIDENT

Huskisson Memorial, Parkside

Access

On the eastern side of Parkside Road, about a quarter of a mile south of the junction with the A572. Best viewed from the road bridge.

This memorial was erected in 1930 on the centenary of the opening of the Liverpool and Manchester Railway, and commemorates the death of William Huskisson, the Liverpool MP.

On the opening day of the railway, 15 September 1830, a number of trains were run from Liverpool towards Manchester carrying official dignitaries. William Huskisson was on one of these. The trains stopped at Parkside to take on water, and after other trains had already departed some fifty passengers started to alight while the remaining engines were filled.

At the moment of the accident Huskisson was talking to the Duke of Wellington, but failed to notice a train approaching in the same direction on the parallel track. Huskisson's left leg was severed. With great speed he was put on one of the trains and carried on the line to Eccles at the then unheard of speed of 35mph. Despite medical attention, he died several hours later.

See also Huskisson's memorial and grave in Liverpool's St James's Park (page 31).

A Bridge 'of Very Curious and Beautiful Construction'

Rainhill Skew Bridge, Liverpool and Manchester Railway

This bridge, carrying the Liverpool to Manchester turnpike road over the Liverpool and Manchester Railway, was described when first built as 'of very curious and beautiful construction' and one of the 'most remarkable skew bridges in the kingdom'.

Built at an angle of 34 degrees to the railway tracks, it was the most acute of the fifteen skew bridges built on the railway. The Liverpool docks engineer, Jesse Hartley, is considered to be the probable designer of the bridge, as he was familiar with a bridge at Lancaster, on which certain aspects of the design were based.

Work started on the bridge at the end of 1828 with George Findlay as contractor. A full-sized wooden framework model was erected in an adjoining field, and the stone blocks used to build the bridge were cut, dressed and numbered in advance. Each was individually shaped. The bridge was then built, being completed by June 1829. The total cost was £3,735.

The distance between the bridge parapets at road level was originally 30ft, but the width was increased by 4ft on the southern side in 1903. Stone tablets on each side of the bridge record George Stephenson as the engineer and Charles Lawrence as the chairman of the company.

The famous Rainhill Locomotive Trials took place a quarter of a mile to the east of the bridge between 6 and 14 October 1829.

Access

In the centre of Rainhill, on the Warrington Road (A57), best viewed from the station platform.

An exhibition about the trials can be seen at the nearby Rainhill Library, on View Road.

A CHURCH NAMED AFTER ITS FOUNDER

St Bartholomew's Church, Rainhill

Access

On the northern side of Warrington Road (A57) at the junction with Chapel Lane.

This elaborate neo-classical church, built in red sandstone and complete with tower and entrance gateway, was built by Bartholomew Bretherton at a cost of £4,000. It was consecrated on 24 August 1840 and is officially dedicated to the Apostle Bartholomew.

Bretherton was a self-made man who had profited greatly by running a coaching service from Liverpool to Manchester and London in the early years of the nineteenth century. He built a mansion for himself and his family in Rainhill in 1824, which is now the adjacent Loyola Hall. Rainhill was the first stop on the coach journey out of Liverpool.

A tower was added in 1849. In 1883 the imposing entrance gateway was added by Mrs Mary Stapleton-Bretherton, the founder's daughter. The interior of the church was remodelled in 1886. The church was substantially reordered and redecorated in the mid-1980s with the aim of restoring the simplicity of its original layout. It was re-dedicated on 17 March 1985 by Derek Worlock, Archbishop of Liverpool.

5

CURIOSITIES
OF WIRRAL

A NEW TRADITIONAL TRAMWAY SYSTEM

Birkenhead Tramway

Access

The best place to catch the tram is at the Woodside Ferry Terminal.

There may no longer be any trams to Lime Street or to the Pier Head, but Birkenhead once again has a tramway running to the Woodside Ferry terminal.

Birkenhead was the first place in Europe that had a street tramway, which opened on 29 August 1860 on a route from Woodside to Birkenhead Park. The system, which was horse drawn, was the brainchild of a flamboyant and appropriately named American, George Francis Train. It is said that Jules Verne's fictitious character, Phileas Fogg, from the book *Around the World in Eighty Days*, was based on Train. Birkenhead's tramways were converted to electric traction in 1901, but finally closed in July 1937, when the trams were replaced by buses.

The current tramway, established in 1995, is a tourist route running from Woodside Ferry Terminal, along Shore Road, to the Old Colonial pub at the tram depot on Taylor Street, where guided tours are available. Utilising a short stretch of street running, it passes Egerton Bridge, a bascule bridge dating from 1847, which has displays about the local dock system and a viewing platform. Originally the line was to have run in a loop via Conway Park and Hamilton Square, but the scheme was cut back when money became short.

A number of preserved trams from Birkenhead, Wallasey and Liverpool are run on the line. Two modern trams also run, one of which is pictured above. These were built in 1992 in Hong Kong to a traditional double-deck design that had been running in that city since 1948. They have both been given fleet numbers that follow on directly from the highest number in the old fleet which existed at the time of the closure of the town's system in 1937.

ADULT

BIRKENHEAD TRAMWAYS

Not transferable

RETURN TRAM RIDE

Trams operated by the Metropolitan Borough of Wirral

AT 03 03876

See also the former Birkenhead horse tram on static display within the ferry terminal.

HOME OF THE 'GIANT GRASSHOPPER'

Shore Road Pumping Station, Birkenhead

Access

On Hamilton
Street, between
Shore Road and
Canning Street.
Open weekends
only.

This building is home to the 'Giant Grasshopper', a type of steam-powered beam engine where one end of the beam is pivoted, allowing the other end to move vertically 'grasshopper-like' some 15ft. A counter balance consisting of a second beam with a weighted end containing 20 tons of pig iron was provided beneath the floor of the building.

The pump, manufactured in the 1870s by Andrew Barclay of Kilmarnock, is designed to extract water from the Mersey rail tunnels. A total of 3,500 gallons of water per minute could be pumped. The engine weighed over 260 tons and was one of three on the railway, another being located in Birkenhead and one in George's Dock in Liverpool. The pump was used for about seventy-five years before it was replaced by two electric ones housed in the same building. The original boilers for the pump were removed long ago and it is now powered by a hydraulic cylinder below the counter-balance beam.

LOCATED IN ONE OF THE FINEST GEORGIAN SQUARES IN BRITAIN

Former Birkenhead Town Hall, Hamilton Square

Access

On the eastern side of Hamilton Square. The museum is open Tuesday to Sundays.

This imposing classical building, now Wirral Museum, was designed by local architect Charles Ellison in 1882, and was opened by John Laird in February 1887. It cost £43,067 to build and is reputedly based on the Town Hall in Bolton. The clock in the 200ft high clock tower was started by Elsie Laird, daughter of the mayor, on 27 November 1886. The building was extensively damaged by fire in July 1901 after which it was necessary to rebuild the tower.

After the local government reorganisation of 1974, the building did not become the headquarters of the new Wirral local authority, but remained in use as council offices until 1990/91, before being restored as the museum. The interior of the building is superb and is well worth a visit, with a splendid main staircase and sumptuous late High Victorian stained-glass windows. The displays include a model of Woodside as it was in June 1934.

The old Town Hall was the last building to be built in Hamilton Square, designed by the Edinburgh architect Gillespie Graham, and built in the years 1825 to 1847. The square was commissioned by William Laird, the founder of the Birkenhead Iron works, later Cammel Laird, as part of a town development scheme, reflected in the gridiron pattern of nearby streets, at one time referred to as 'The City of the Future'. The square is built of local Storeton stone. Although perfectly proportioned, it is said that no two sides are identical. When built it was described as being 'scarcely excelled by any in the kingdom', although the similarities to squares in Edinburgh's New Town, cannot be discounted. Its central gardens were originally for residents only.

THE PARK ON WHICH NEW YORK'S CENTRAL PARK WAS BASED

Birkenhead Park

Access

On the south
side of Park
Road North
(A553), half a
mile west of the
town centre.

Birkenhead Park is one of the first public parks in the UK and the first to be funded by a local authority. The idea of such a park had first been mooted in 1841, and in 1843 the town's Improvement Commissioners bought 185 acres of marshy ground, some 125 for the park proper and the rest for building development, out of which the park's costs would be recovered.

In August 1843 the noted landscape gardener Joseph Paxton was engaged to design and construct the park for a fee of £800. Development of the park was completed in 1846 with the official opening on 5 April 1847 by Sir William Jackson, who had been instrumental in getting the project completed.

It is one of Paxton's most important works. His overall concept was to create an idealised landscape of meadows and woodlands. Features such as the boathouse and Swiss bridge form viewpoints across the long and winding lakes. Many of the buildings, including most of the entrance lodges, were the work of Lewis Hornblower, the young architect from Liverpool, who was later to be involved with Sefton Park (see page 61).

The main lodge, shown here, however, was the work of Gillespie Graham, the designer of Hamilton Square. It is some 125ft high, with an entrance span 16ft high and 43ft wide. Intended to be a grand triumphal arch, it has been likened to Marble Arch and the Arc de Triomphe in Paris.

The park was visited in 1850 by the American F.L. Olmstead, as part of a tour of Europe. Olmstead later borrowed some of Paxton's ideas for the design of New York's Central Park. He is reported as having said 'In democratic America there was nothing to be thought of as comparable with this People's Garden'.

Paxton's original design remains largely intact, and although the park has suffered in recent decades from vandalism and cut-backs in local authority spending, its status was recognised in 1977 when it was declared a Conservation Area and in 1995 when English Heritage awarded it Grade I listed landscape status.

Restoration started on a piecemeal basis in the late 1980s. In 2002 a grant of £7.4 million was awarded from the Heritage Lottery Fund, and a comprehensive restoration scheme is in progress. A new glass pavilion providing an exhibition and interpretation centre, teaching areas and café is, at the time of writing, under construction.

A MEMORIAL TO AN EISTEDDFOD NOT HELD IN WALES

Eisteddfod Commemoration Stone, Birkenhead Park

Liverpool and Birkenhead, being relatively close to Wales, have both been natural destinations for many Welsh people seeking work, so much so that at one time Liverpool was unofficially called the 'Capital of North Wales'. It is not surprising, therefore, that the Royal National Eisteddfod, that annual celebration of Welsh culture and language, has been held at times in both Liverpool and Birkenhead, the last such occasion being in 1929.

This rough granite slab, commemorates the best known outside Wales Eisteddfod, which was held in Birkenhead Park in September 1917. The stone was a gift of local builder Councillor David Evans.

The event is associated with soldier-poet Ellis Humphrey Evans, better known as Hedd Wynn (1887–1917) who had enlisted early in 1917 into the Royal Welsh Fusiliers. Before leaving home he had already begun his work *Yr Arwr* (The Hero), which was finished when he spent time at Litherland, and later posted from France for entry in the Eisteddfod. His pseudonym, Fleur de Lis, was called out (as the winner) at the Eisteddfod on 6 September, but he had already been killed on 31 July at the Battle of Pilken Ridge. The bardic chair he would have been awarded, also provided by David Evans, was then named as the Black Chair, and the event is known as the Eisteddfod of the Black Chair.

The stone was restored by Birkenhead's Welsh community in 1957, and overlooks the site where the Eisteddfod was held. News reports in late 2004 raised the possibility of the Eisteddfod being held again in Liverpool.

> Birkenhead's Central Library contains a fine modern stained-glass window commemorating another First World War soldier-poet, Wilfred Owen, who lived for a time in the town.

THE FINAL VOYAGE OF THIS SUBMARINE WILL REMAIN UNKNOWN

Historic Warships at Birkenhead

This rusty submarine is the German *U-534*, the only German U-Boat to be raised from the seabed after being sunk by the Allies in the Second World War. It is open to the public, although pre-bookings on tours are necessary and children under twelve are not permitted on the vessel. She was sunk on 5 May 1945 and was the last U-Boat to leave Germany in the war. Whether she was heading for South America or carrying treasure to support escaped Nazis will never be known, as it is said there is no one still alive who has such knowledge. She is currently on loan to the museum from Danish owners Den Bla Avis, who salvaged her in 1993.

U-534 is one of five warships that form the basis of this very interesting museum formed in the early 1990s by the Warship Preservation Trust. It is the only such museum in the UK to hold a collection of twentieth-century warships. Two of the ships are comparatively modern vessels which took part in the Falklands War of 1981/82.

HMS *Onyx* was the only conventionally powered submarine of the Royal Navy that served in the Falklands. Her job was to land special forces close to the shore where they could disembark using rubber boats or canoes. Because of her small size she was nicknamed 'the Sardine's Revenge'. The frigate HMS *Plymouth* saw the surrender of South Georgia by the Argentine forces, signed in her wardroom.

The wooden-hulled Ton class minesweeper HMS *Bronington*, launched in 1953, was commanded by HRH The Prince of Wales between February and December 1976, during his period of active service with the Royal Navy. From 1992 to 2003 the ship had been on display in Trafford Park, on the Manchester Ship Canal.

The latest addition to the museum's fleet is Landing Craft-Tank LCT *7074*, which took part in the Normandy landings in 1944. She is not currently accessible and requires major restoration, for which grant applications have been made.

Access

On the south side of Dock Road (A5139). Open daily most of the year. Admission charge payable.

THE 'BACK-TO-FRONT' TOWN HALL

Wallasey Town Hall

Access

On the eastern side of Brighton Street (A554).

This imposing building is the former Wallasey Town Hall, now the main offices of Wirral Metropolitan Borough. It was built with its most impressive frontage facing the River Mersey, with a fine staircase leading down to the promenade that runs along the river at this point. The frontage to Brighton Street is comparatively modest.

The choice of this site was a long drawn-out affair, referred to locally at the time as 'The Battle of the Sites'. Some four sites were under consideration. The foundation stone of the building was laid in March 1914, with construction in the hands of Moss & Sons. The First World War effectively delayed its use as a town hall, and it was used as a military hospital from August 1916. Holding some 300 beds, about 3,500 men were treated there. The building finally became Wallasey's Town Hall officially on 3 November 1920.

The Town Hall is built in a fairly nondescript area midway between the Seacombe Ferry and the former Egremont Ferry, which ended in 1946, both of which used to be Wallasey's main connecting points with Liverpool.

At the foot of the steps, inlaid into the Promenade, is 'Games', a patchwork of twelve cast-bronze roundels arranged in a grid reflecting the formality of the nearby Town Hall. In the centre of each roundel is a disc lit by fibre-optic cables. Children from Elleray Park School were involved in the design of the scheme, which was implemented as part of Wirral 2000 project.

About half a mile north of the Town Hall, on the Promenade, is the site of the old Egremont Ferry, with the Ferry Inn. This part of the Promenade has been known as Wallasey's 'Speakers Corner' for some time, but its use for such purposes now appears limited.

A STATUE OF A LADY CONNECTED WITH SMUGGLING

Mother Redcap, *Liscard*

Access

On the pedestrianised Liscard Way.

This statue by Robert Stocker, erected in 1996, commemorates one of the area's notorious and colourful characters.

On the Promenade at Egremont, between Lincoln Grove and Caithness Drive, formerly stood a building called Mother Redcap's. Built in 1595, this building, comprising a combined café and public house, owed its name to its proprietor, Polly Jones, also known as Mother Redcap, after the red cap or bonnet she habitually wore, who lived in the 1770s. Its relatively isolated position at the time, on the river bank and the only building between Seacombe and New Brighton, extensive cellars and caves supposedly connecting the building to other parts of the nearby coast made the pub a centre of the local smuggling trade, which thrived on the wrecking opportunities present along the northern coast of Wirral peninsula.

Mother Redcap, a widow, was a very likeable character and very popular with sailors, helping to keep them protected from the various press gangs that abounded at the time. She was reputedly the central figure in all this illicit activity, acting as 'banker' to all the various protagonists until her death in her eighties.

The sculpture shows Mother Redcap shielding herself with a cloak, and two sailors, Charlie and Gerard, taking the goods away and keeping a look-out for the Customs men.

The original Mother Redcap's closed as a pub in 1862. It was rebuilt and became a house in 1888, but reverted to a café at a later date. By the 1960s it was derelict, and after vandalism it was demolished in 1974. The site is currently occupied by Mother Redcap's Nursing Home.

A BOOT GIVEN AS A REWARD

Leather Boot, The Boot Inn, Wallasey

Access

On the south side of Wallasey Road (A551), to the west of Liscard, at the junction with Newton Road. The boot is located in a glass case to the right of the main bar.

Our Good Queen Bess did rule the realm when honest Jack was hoaste upon this inn, well helped by lusty wife and bucksome daughter Joan.

One wild dark night when all were snoring snug abed, a fierce wild horseman, bedaubed with muck and blood did gallop to the door, making a thunderous rump thereon; when our hoaste did open unto him, he rushed into the house, a big jack boot in one hand, and a great house pistol in t'other, calling wild foul words for instant meat and drink.

He had a beastly savage look, and our hoaste did eye him well while meat and drink went bolling down his wolfish maw. Thinks Jack, there's booty in that boot, for when he thumped it on the board there was a clink of gold, the pistol too was bye. Our honest Jack was 'cute and bold' and when he brought more wine he spilt it on the man, and when he turned in wrath Jack whipped the pistol to his scounce and called for his lusty wife and bucksome Joan, and they did bind the robber safe and secure, and make the gold lined boot secure.

This scarce well done when three gentlemen, one with bloody scounce and bootless leg, who when he saw the robber bound was glad, but soon began to wave his boot. Now our hoaste begin to now and bid his man bring the gold lined boot. The gentleman was then in hearty mood and gave ten guineas to our hoaste, ten more to lusty wife and bucksome Joan. He gave the robber to the gibbet and the boot to be a sign unto this inn while it doth stand.

The original inn was in fact demolished in 1925 and the current building rebuilt behind it in order to allow the main road to be widened at this point. It is not known how much truth there is in the story above, which is written beside the glass case in which the boot is currently kept.

THRICE BURNT, TWICE A CHURCH WITHOUT A TOWER AND ONCE A TOWER WITHOUT A CHURCH

St Hilary's Church, Wallasey

St Hilary's Church is located on one of the highest points in Wirral. It is unusual in having two towers, one clearly older than the rest of the church, and separated from it. It is thought that this has been the site of a church since the sixth century, and one certainly existed at the time of the Norman Conquest, after which the church was rebuilt several times.

The isolated tower bears the date 1530, although the rest of the church was rebuilt in about 1760 using the same materials. The church was destroyed in a fire in the early hours of Sunday 31 January 1857, only a few years after it had been extensively restored. The cause of the blaze was fires lit the previous evening to heat up the church. The flues became overheated – some say because of over enthusiastic stoking after parishioners had complained of the cold – and caused the church's wooden flooring to catch fire.

It is reported that the church received £2,000 from its insurers in respect of the loss. It was also rumoured that the church tower was used to store contraband, and that the flames had a blue haze from burning brandy which could be seen as far away as the Welsh coast. In fact, the peculiar colour was caused by burning fat from bacons that had been left hanging in the tower. The current building was built between 1858 and 1859 from local stone quarried at Rake Lane.

Access

On the hill above Wallasey Village, at the junction of Claremont Road and Broadway.

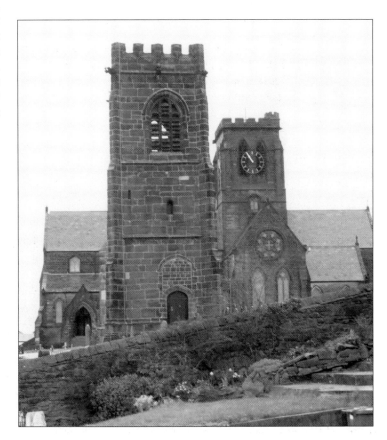

THIS SCHOOL ONCE HELD EIGHTY-THREE CHILDREN

Former Wallasey Grammar School building

Access

On the northern side of Breck Road (B5145).

The Metropolitan Borough of Wirral is one of the few local authorities to retain a grammar school system. One of its schools, Wallasey Grammar, has origins as far back as 1595. From 1656 it had been located in the old Wallasey parish church of St Hilary's.

The small sandstone building dates from 1799 and was erected by public subscription. All teaching would have been the responsibility of one man, and all ages, both girls and boys, would have been taught in the school. At one time it is said that this simple building held up to eighty-three pupils.

Growing demands from an expanding population led to the school moving to St George's Road in January 1864 and then to Withens Lane in Liscard in 1873. The school was rebuilt at that site in 1911, the buildings now being used by Liscard Primary School. The grammar school moved to its present site in Leasowe in 1967. The former Prime Minister, the late Harold Wilson, was an old boy of Wallasey Grammar.

THE 'SNAKE IN THE GRASS' FORT

Liscard Battery

Access

At the junction of Magazine Lane and Magazine Brow, which are to the east of Seabank Road (A554).

Liscard Battery and the Liscard Magazines are often mistaken for each other, but both were separate institutions, existing on adjoining sites at different dates.

The Liscard Magazine was not a military installation, but had been established by Liverpool Corporation in the 1750s as a place for storing gunpowder imported into the city. Until 1751 this had been done at a powder magazine on Clarence Street, but growth of the city meant that carrying gunpowder through the streets was becoming dangerous. The magazine was sited between Magazine Lane and Fort Street covered and approximately 1 acre. After being substantially extended in 1838 it comprised a series of separate chambers divided from each other by mounds of earth. The whole was surrounded by a wall, a thick plantation, and then by a further wall.

In 1851 it was reported that some 14,000 barrels of gunpowder were being stored in the magazine. Its presence within a rapidly growing residential area became a concern and in that year an Act of Parliament was obtained which obliged Liverpool to give up the magazine, after which the gunpowder was stored on old ship hulks located between New Ferry and Eastham. Today little is evident of the magazine apart from the old watchmen's hut, a small circular building at the lower end of Fort Street, now incorporated into a private house.

On the other side of the road (pictured right) is the old entrance gateway to Liscard Battery. This was built in 1858 and was a 'masked battery', known as 'the snake in the grass' to local inhabitants, deliberately built among housing to avoid detection from enemy ships travelling up the Mersey. It housed seven 10in guns and was manned by a small garrison of the 55th Royal Artillery.

The battery was soon obsolete in military terms and its occupation had ended well before it was declared surplus to requirements and sold to the Liverpool Yacht Club in 1912 for £1,620. Subsequent development has seen housing built on the site, and only this entrance gateway and some of the perimeter walls remain.

The 'Little Gibraltar of the Mersey'

Fort Perch, New Brighton

Access

To the north of the Marine Promenade. The fort and museum are open daily (admission charge payable).

This fort is thought to have been the most important coastal defence battery in the north-west of England. It is a Grade II listed building. Intended to protect the port of Liverpool from the Napoleonic threat, it cost some £26,965 when built between 1826 and 1829.

Built from red Runcorn sandstone, its walls are between 24ft and 32ft high, with the towers 40ft high. The fort was built on what was known locally as Black Rock, and originally had 18 guns, accommodation for 100 men, and a magazine and storerooms at a sunken level in the central courtyard. Because of the importance of the installation, it was not marked on contemporary Ordnance Survey maps (see below).

Over the years the armaments and soldiery based at the fort altered. Originally, smooth-bore cannon balls would have been used. Local fishermen were rewarded every time they returned balls to the fort that had been fired during practices. In

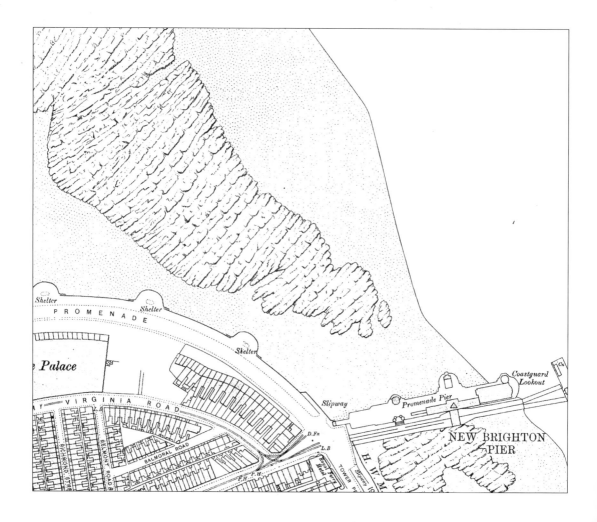

later years heavier guns were installed. In 1893 they were removed and later replaced by three 6in naval guns. The final armament of the fort when it closed in 1954 was two 6in guns and two machine guns.

During the Second World War, it was camouflaged to look like a tea garden from the air, with paths and painted lawns, and the word 'TEAS' painted on the roof. After 1954 the fort passed through several private owners and it gradually became derelict. Restoration started in 1976 when a new owner took over, and the fort is now open to the public.

The fort only ever fired its guns in anger twice. In the First World War warning shots were fired across the bows of a Norwegian fishing vessel, which was unaware that war had been declared. Both shots were wide of their mark. The first shot landed in the sandhills at Crosby. It was recovered and finished up in the Officers Mess of the Seaforth Battery, bearing the words 'A present from New Brighton'. The second shot hit the bows of a ship at anchor. At the start of the Second World War a similar incident occurred when a fishing smack tried to enter the port through the Rock Channel, which had been closed to shipping, some 15 minutes after war had been declared. In this instance the unfortunate owner of the vessel was obliged to pay £25 for each round fired.

A GUIDE DOG ON THE SITE OF 'HAM AND EGGS PARADE'

Guide Dog statue, New Brighton

Access

On the south side of Marine Promenade close to the Floral Pavilion Theatre.

This small statue of a guide dog commemorates the founding of the Guide Dog for the Blind Association in New Brighton in 1931. New Brighton today is clean and attractive. It has acres of free car parking. Helpful information boards have much to say about the place and its history. It has many visitors, but not the large numbers who patronised it in the days when it was a popular seaside resort, a status it kept as recently as the 1970s but which it has now lost completely. Controversial proposals for development of the town's seafront area were being hotly debated in mid-2005.

New Brighton's heyday saw it attracting many day trippers who came on the ferries that operated from Liverpool until 1972. A tower, built to rival that at Blackpool, stood until the First World War, and its ballroom survived until 1969.

At the heart of the promenade was the parade of shops and tea rooms, built between 1872 and 1873, called Aquarium Terrace but unofficially known as Ham and Egg Parade, or Tea Pot Row, after the many tawdry eating houses, fortune tellers and shooting galleries which stretched along the front where the guide dog statue and adjoining gardens now stand. As well as street hawkers and pickpockets, the area's bad reputation also arose from various dubious activities carried out in the upper rooms. The reputation of the parade was quite unlike the rest of the town, and there was general approval when demolition was proposed in 1906.

FORMERLY ONE OF THE BIG ATTRACTIONS OF OLD NEW BRIGHTON

Red Noses and Yellow Noses Rocks, New Brighton

Access

Via the gates on Portland Street, off King's Parade (A554).

The coastline in the immediate vicinity of New Brighton was altered in the nineteenth and twentieth centuries and land reclamation has left the original shoreline several hundred yards inland. Towards the western end of the town are several outcrops of brightly coloured sandstone, called Red Noses and Yellow Noses respectively, which were formerly a favourite venue for picnickers, whose children would clamber over their nooks and crannies.

The Noses contain caves, unfortunately now blocked up, said to have been used by smugglers, and linked with Mother Redcap's (see page 131) in Egremont a mile away and St Hilary's Church in Wallasey. These rumours were disproved in the years following the Second World War when the caves were opened up and found to only extend some 200yds. Internal access is still possible via trapdoors in the gardens of the houses on the cliff tops, and the caves are said to contain graffiti dating back to the seventeenth century. The early history of the caves remains a matter of conjecture.

The Noses, New Brighton

AN ENERGY-EFFICIENT BUILDING FROM 1961

Solar Campus

Access

On the south side of Leasowe Road (A551), to the west of the junction with the A554.

Originally known as St George's School, this energy-efficient building was way ahead of its time when built in 1961. It was designed by Emslie Morgan, who had made extensive studies into ways of harnessing the sun's rays as a way of cutting heating costs.

Solar Campus is windowless on the north side and completely glazed on the south, with some 10,000 sq. ft of glass, held in aluminium frames built in two layers 2ft apart. The school also features a very thick roof, walls covered with slabs of plastic foam and excellent sealing treatment to openings.

In winter a temperature of at least 60 degrees Fahrenheit is maintained inside as the glass panels harness the ultra-violet rays from the available sunshine. In summer the solar wall can be modified to deflect or absorb the heat by manual operation of vents at each floor level, and there are wind scoops within the glass cavity modifying the air flow. In typical British tradition, it is a good idea that apparently has rarely, if ever, been copied.

THIS HOTEL CONTAINS A 'STAR CHAMBER'

Leasowe Castle

Access

On the northern side of Leasowe Road (A551). Best viewed from the North Wirral Coastal Path. Readers should not enter the hotel grounds unless they are *bona fide* users of the hotel.

This interesting-looking building has its origins in 1593, when New Hall was built by Ferdinando, the 5th Earl of Derby. It is thought that it was not built as a traditional castle but merely as a secure residence for its owner. An oft-repeated theory that it was built as a viewing lodge for the well-known Wallasey Races, predecessor to the present-day Derby, is now considered unlikely.

The original building was an octagonal tower, built with its entrance door 5ft above ground level to give both security and protection from high tides. The walls were 3ft thick. A later owner, thought to be William, the 6th Earl, added four turrets to the tower. However, after a period of use as a farmhouse the building had been abandoned by the end of the seventeenth century, by which time it was known as Mockbeggar Hall.

In 1802 the ruin was bought by Mrs Margaret Boode, daughter of the Revd Thomas Danneth, Rector of Liverpool, and the widow of a wealthy West Indian plantation owner. She renamed it Leasowe Castle and spent a considerable amount on it, partly to aid her in her work of assisting shipwrecked sailors, for which she was renowned.

After her death in 1826 the property passed to her daughter, Mary Anne, who had married Colonel Edward Cust, later Queen Victoria's Master of Ceremonies, in 1821. He undertook further alterations and a period of use as a hotel followed until 1843, when he took up residence. In 1836, when the old Exchequer Buildings at Westminster were being demolished, he arranged for the oak panelling from the old Star Chamber to be saved to line the ground-floor dining room of the castle. This room subsequently acquired the name Star Chamber on account of the ceiling of gilded stars on a pale background.

Another of his additions is the Battle Staircase, so named because of the painted nameplates of famous British battles, complete with dates, the commanding general and reigning Sovereign of the time, set into the handrails.

The building again became a hotel, called the Leasowe Castle Hotel, in 1891. The castle was used as a railway convalescent home between 1911 and 1970, apart from a brief period in the First World War when it housed prisoners of war. It was bought by the local authority in 1974, and a period of neglect followed before it was sold to the current owner in 1980, who has restored the property and brought it back into use as a hotel.

THE OLDEST LIGHTHOUSE IN ENGLAND

Leasowe Lighthouse

Access

Along the road
that leads
through Leasowe
Common, about
a quarter of a
mile west of the
turn in the A591
when Leasowe
Road becomes
Pasture Road. It
is open to the
public on certain
Sundays.

This lighthouse was built in 1763 by the Liverpool Corporation Docks Committee. Over the entrance a plaque is inscribed with the initials MWG, representing the Mayor of Liverpool, William Gregson. It was originally known as the Upper Mockbeggar lighthouse, after this part of the coast which is called Mockbeggar Wharf.

The building was built with 660,000 hand-made bricks and is over 100ft tall. The walls are several feet thick, and it is said that because of the marshy ground the foundations comprise cotton bales rescued from a wrecked ship. There are seven floors, reached by a cast-iron staircase with 130 steps. The light consisted at first of an open coal fire, until a lantern with three burners was installed in 1772.

Originally two lighthouses were built at this point. Another, a 'lower light', was built a quarter of a mile out to sea, but was destroyed by a storm in 1769.

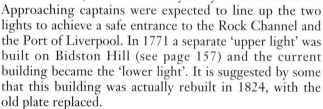

Approaching captains were expected to line up the two lights to achieve a safe entrance to the Rock Channel and the Port of Liverpool. In 1771 a separate 'upper light' was built on Bidston Hill (see page 157) and the current building became the 'lower light'. It is suggested by some that this building was actually rebuilt in 1824, with the old plate replaced.

The lighthouse was last used on 14 July 1908, by which time a buoy system was in operation on the Mersey. After closure the building was used as a tea room by the last keeper, Mrs Williams, until her death in 1935. In 1929 it was offered for sale, but found no takers until bought by Wallasey Corporation in 1930 for £900.

In 1973 the building was painted white, but otherwise continued to deteriorate until 1989, when it was refurbished by Wirral Borough Council, which opened a small visitor centre on the ground floor. A Friends of Leasowe Lighthouse group was formed the same year, and a new roof and internal steps soon followed. Access to the top became possible in 1996.

Although no memorial to this remains, Moreton saw Britain's first public hovercraft service, which ran to Rhyl between July and September 1962. The experimental service was provided with a Vickers VA3 hovercraft operated by British United Airways Ltd the managing director at the time was one Freddie Laker. Hoylake was to have been the original starting point, but Moreton was chosen after Hoylake residents feared that the service would attract too many visitors. The service ran some 172 trips and carried some 3,700 passengers.

A TRIBUTE TO A LOCAL GRAND NATIONAL WINNER

Shop Name plates, Moreton Cross

These small plaques are visible at first-floor height above the shops at this busy road junction. Containing names such as Spring Gate, Golden Valley and Sweet Cecil, they are the names of Grand National racehorses from long ago.

The plaques were placed here by local jockey F. ('Titch') Mason, who built the shops as an investment, and who rode each of the horses in the Grand National at various times. He rode in the Grand National twelve times, and one horse, Kirkland, took him to victory in 1905. His house, also called Kirkland, was located on Pasture Road.

Access

On the south side of the junction between Hoylake Road (A553) and Upton Road (A551).

On the other side of the road junction is an imposing public house, the Coach and Horses. Dating from 1928, it is locally known as The Cathedral in view of its mock turrets, half timbering and sandstone walls.

HOYLAKE'S LANDLOCKED LIGHTHOUSE

Former Hoylake Upper Light

Access

Best viewed from either Valencia Road or Warren Road.

This lighthouse was one of a pair built in 1764. This one was built of brick while the other (or lower) lighthouse, on Alderley Road, was 24ft high and built of wood so that it could be moved to accommodate tide and sand movements.

Both were replaced in 1865, the new upper light being some 55ft tall with nineteen rooms. It was necessary to acquire surrounding properties to prevent encroachment by housing, reducing the effectiveness of the lighthouse. The light was provided by coal fires and the installation was the first to be fitted with special mirrors.

The lighthouse was last used on 14 May 1886 and has since been incorporated into housing. The old lower light was used until 1908, then becoming the entrance to the old Lighthouse Pavilion Theatre. The lighthouse was demolished in December 1922.

A MEMORIAL TO A REMARKABLE DOG

Tell's Tower, West Kirby

Access

At the southern
end of South
Parade, close to
the junction with
Sandy Lane. Best
viewed from the
beach.

This small sandstone tower was built by the Revd John Cumming McDona (or McDonald) in the grounds of his residence, Hilbre House. McDona, born in 1826, had a remarkably varied career during his life. He was rector of Cheadle from 1874 to 1882, a barrister from 1889 and the Conservative MP for Rotherhithe from 1892 to 1906. He died in 1907.

He was also a noted breeder of dogs, especially Alsatians. Tell's Tower, built between 1871 and 1874, commemorates Tell, a rough-coated Mount St Bernard, who died while saving his master from drowning on 22 January 1871, aged seven years. Tell had won all the principal prizes for Alsatians since being imported into the UK in March 1863.

At the base is a carving of the dog, now unfortunately deteriorated owing to weathering of the soft sandstone. An inscription describes Tell as being 'majestic in appearance and noble in character, affectionate in disposition and of undoubted courage'.

In later years the tower was used for storage, as a lookout post during the Second World War, and then by the Girl Guides. Hilbre House in later years was inhabited by the one-time Chancellor of the Exchequer, Selwyn Lloyd, but was demolished some years ago. The tower has now been incorporated into a modern dwelling, one of a number built on the site, and close access is not possible.

A COLUMN PROVIDED AS AID FOR SHIPPING

Mariners' Column, West Kirby

Access

On the western side of Column Road (A540), close to Beacon Road.

This 60ft high classical Doric column, surmounted by a large stone ball, is made of the local red sandstone and is located on what arguably is the finest viewpoint in Wirral. It was erected in 1841 after an earlier windmill, a valuable landmark for sailors, had been destroyed by a gale in 1839. The column, sometimes called the Mariners Beacon, was built by the trustees of the Liverpool Docks on land provided by local landowner John Shaw Leigh, who laid the foundation stone on 16 April 1841. The area of open space in which the column is located is called Liberty Park, so called after the former right of local ratepayers to be able to quarry stone from there to use in house repairs.

A REMARKABLE LOCAL MUSEUM

Charles Dawson Brown Museum, West Kirby

This little museum is situated in a single room comprising the left-hand part of the old sandstone Parochial School building shown in the photograph, which today forms part of the local primary school. It comprises an interesting collection of local items relating to the church and the parish, including many fragments from the different churches that have existed on the site prior to the present building.

Charles Dawson Brown (1829–90) was a wealthy Liverpool cotton broker who lived in West Kirby. He was an avid local historian, school governor and a 'Friend of the Poor'. After his death a public subscription raised funds for a memorial window in the parish church and for the establishment of the museum for his extensive collection of relics, which opened in November 1892. One of the earliest and most important items is a Viking 'hogsback' grave cover, which after restoration has now been put on display in the adjacent church. The museum has had a chequered history over the years, but it was officially reopened by the Hoylake Historical Society in June 1972.

Access

At the end of St Bridget's Lane. The museum has no regular opening hours, and access is by special arrangement with the authorities at St Bridget's Church (donation appreciated). The church itself is open Wednesday to Friday afternoons.

THIS BUILDING COULD CONVEY MESSAGES 'FASTER THAN THE WIND'

Former Telegraph station, Hilbre

The small grassy island known as Hilbre Island, extending to about 11½ acres, is a fascinating place with a long history. There is evidence of settlement on the island during Saxon times. Until the Dissolution of the Monasteries it housed a small cell of monks from Chester Abbey. In 1856 it was bought by the Mersey Docks and Harbour Board, and in 1945 it passed into local authority ownership for the use of the public and as a bird sanctuary, in which use it remains today.

The unusual building (pictured), sometimes called The Pilot's Lookout, is the former telegraph station erected by the Liverpool Docks Trustees in 1841, as part

of a signalling relay system, established in 1827, that stretched from Holyhead to Liverpool. The round objects in the windows are binnacles which supported telescopes from which the adjacent stations on Bidston Hill and Voel Nant near Prestatyn could be observed.

The telegraph system was revolutionary at the time, replacing earlier less accurate flag systems. It is said that it was capable of sending a message all the way from Holyhead to Liverpool and back in just 23 seconds, or 'faster than the wind'.

However, it could only be used in daylight and was prone to disruption by the weather.

One story is that a Holyhead telegraphist, irate at being asked to repeat a message, sent the message 'You're stupid' to Liverpool; the reply which came back within minutes was 'You are fired'!

After the advent of the electric telegraph in 1861 the telegraph station was retained and adapted with instruments for the new system. It ceased to be used sometime after the Second World War. In the past few years it has been restored by the Friends of Hilbre, who open it as a visitor centre on certain weekends.

Great care must be taken when visiting Hilbre Island, which is only accessible by foot. The access track across the sands goes from the Dee Lane slipway via the islands known as Little Eye and Middle Hilbre (direct access is dangerous). The 2-mile trip takes at least one hour in each direction, and visitors should aim to complete the trip between successive high water times, setting out at least two hours after high water, and starting the return trip at least three hours before the next high water. Incoming tides come in very quickly. The high water times are available from the Wirral Country Park at Thurstaston. There are no toilet facilities on the island.

See also the nearby Victorian Buoymaster's House, which housed the official responsible for all the navigation buoys in Liverpool Bay, the Mersey and Dee Estuaries, the Telegraph House provided for the telegraph keeper, and the former Seagull Inn.

WHERE LIFEBOATMEN RODE ACROSS THE SANDS TO GET TO THEIR BOAT

Former lifeboat station, Hilbre

Access

At the northern end of the island.

The Hilbre lifeboat station was built in 1849 at a cost of £1,200. Its purpose was to supplement the Hoylake lifeboat which could not be launched at low tide. When in use, the Hoylake crew either ran or rode across the sands on horseback to get to Hilbre.

The crew were summoned until 1890 by the firing of small cannon, which was later replaced by rockets. The keeper of the telegraph house on Hilbre would ensure that the doors of the lifeboat station were opened so that the boat, which was powered only by oars and a small sail, could be launched without delay.

The station was last used in 1938 when the Hoylake station started to use a diesel-powered tractor to launch their own boat, and the time-consuming trip to Hilbre became unnecessary. It was maintained until June 1939 as a back-up facility but is now derelict, apart from the small tide gauge used to plot the levels of the surrounding waters to aid the navigation of large ships entering Liverpool.

The rest of Hilbre island is well worth exploration if you have the time, with other interesting buildings and remnants of the island's past. A few private dwellings remain, and there is a bird observatory. Over towards the Welsh coast, on West Hoyle Bank, a large colony of Atlantic Grey Seals can often be seen.

THIS BUILDING HAS BEEN MOVED COMPLETELY

Hill Bark, Royden Park

Access

Within the grounds of Royden Park, accessible via Montgomery Hill (B5140) and Hill Bark Road. The property is privately owned and close inspection is not possible without prior arrangement.

The original building on this site was built by Septimus Ledward, who had bought the site in 1865. Constructed of sandstone, it was located on the site of an ancient tithe barn and was named Hill Bark.

In 1930/1 the original Hill Bark was replaced by the park's then owner, Sir Ernest Royden, with the present mock-Tudor building, which had originally been built on Bidston Hill in 1891 by the soap manufacturer R.W. Hudson, and named Bidston Court. The design of its interior courtyard is said to have been influenced by Little Moreton Hall in Cheshire. When it was transported between sites every stone and beam was numbered to aid rebuilding.

The interior of the building is as remarkable as its exterior. There are stained-glass windows by William Morris, many other Arts and Crafts features and the remnants of many former stately homes. A set of double doors to the main dining room came from a tea clipper, while the Jacobean fireplace in the Great Hall is reputedly from Sir Walter Raleigh's former home, dating from 1577. There is also a minstrel's gallery and an organ, which finds use today with the building's current function.

As Bidston Court the building had attracted the attention of the German Kaiser's son in 1911. Local myths state that he built an exact copy of the building

in Potsdam near Berlin, calling it the Cecelianhof in honour of his wife. This is not strictly speaking true, as the building is only partially inspired by Bidston Court. Miraculously, it escaped damage during the Second World War and was used by the Allies for the signing of the Potsdam Agreement in 1945. The Russian Army used it for parties during the Cold War era.

When Sir Ernest died in 1960 Hill Bark was bought by the local authority and turned into an old people's home. It remained as such until 1990, when the home was closed, and in 1995 it was sold for £300,000. For many years, in the summer, plays by Shakespeare were performed in front of the house by the Hillbark Players.

Hill Bark is now in use as a very picturesque location for weddings, when the organ is used, and other social events, and has recently become a small hotel.

Edward Ould, the architect of the building, is reported to have said, 'No style of building will harmonise so quickly with its surroundings. . . . And none continue to live on such terms of good fellowship with other materials. . . .' He was right.

NAMED AFTER THE DANISH GOD THOR

Thor's Stone, Thurstaston Common

This is a popular spot for visitors to the area, being the perfect adventure playground for children. Comprising a large rectangular block of red sandstone, 50ft long, 30ft wide and 25ft high, Thor's Stone was reputedly used as a sacrificial altar by the Danes in honour of Thor, the god of war, its red colour caused by the blood of priests and captives. Set in a hollow, the stone has an irregular surface and the nature of its soft, weathered sandstone has enabled generations of graffiti-writers to make their mark on it. The shape and survival of the stone, in all probability, is due to the fact that the better quality stone surrounding it was quarried away to be used in local buildings and walls.

Access

Located about a quarter of a mile north-west of the western end of School Lane, off Thurstaston Road.

A TOWER HAUNTED BY A LADY IN A WHITE DRESS

Brimstage Hall

Access

On the south side of Brimstage Road (A5137) in the centre of the village. The craft village operates most days and has a car park.

This tower is one of the oldest buildings in Merseyside. It is not known when it was built. Brimstage, or 'Brunstath' as it was once called, was originally held by the Domville family. It passed to the Hulses, when Margery Domville married Sir High Hulse. In 1398 they obtained a licence to build a small chapel or oratory at their home in Brimstage. This probably would have been in the base of the tower. In the south-east corner of this room is a roughly cut stone corbel, said to be an early representation of a Cheshire cat.

Brimstage passed to the Troutbeck family in 1440 by marriage and in 1540 to Sir John Talbot, whose descendants became the Earls of Shrewsbury. William Hesketh Lever acquired it in 1908. Apart from the tower, the original hall was demolished in about 1560 when the present building was erected.

One of the daughters of the Earl of Shrewsbury, Margaret, is reputed to have thrown herself off the top of the tower in 1807 after being disappointed in love. Her ghost, wearing a white dress, is said to haunt the corridors of the building. Nowadays, the whole complex is used as a craft and speciality shopping village.

A REMNANT OF A NINETEENTH-CENTURY FOLLY

Barnston Towers, Heswall

Access

On Barnston Towers Close, off the south side of Barnston Road (A551).

This castellated circular brick tower, together with another, now partly removed, were built as folly decorations to Barnston Towers, a large villa built by J.W. Bourne in about 1884. Despite its name it is not located at Barnston, but on the fringes of Heswall and Gayton. Originally in open countryside, it may have been built in anticipation of the area being opened up by the railways, as the line linking Heswall to West Kirby (now closed) opened in 1886, followed later still by the Bidston to Chester line with its own Heswall (originally Heswall Hills) station. Nikolaus Pevsner claims the property dates from 1852, and was a remodelling of an earlier building on the site.

Recently the main property has been subdivided into flats, and both the former tower and outbuildings now form separate houses. One of the latter was advertised for sale in late 2004 with an asking price of nearly £½ million.

NAMED AFTER A POEM BY ROBERT BURNS

Tam O' Shanter Urban Farm, Bidston

Access

To the west of
Boundary Road
(B5151). The
Urban Farm is
open daily.

This cottage, now at the centre of an urban farm, is thought to have been built by a heath squatter about 300 years ago. In 1837 its occupant was one Richard Lea, a master stonemason and probably a Scotsman. He decided to decorate the building by erecting a carved stone slab on the gable end depicting a scene from the Robert Burns poem 'Tam O'Shanter'. The scene shows

Tam, pursued by witches he has iritated, trying to reach a bridge which the witches would not dare to cross. He did get across the bridge, and the witches, who would not dare cross running water, only caught his poor horse Maggie's tail. Lea also made the weather vane with its animal heads. The building became known as Tam O' Shanter's Cottage as a result of the carving, and became well known in the area. In 1950 it was officially graded as of special interest.

Unfortunately the cottage was mostly destroyed by fire in 1954 and was nearly demolished. It was saved after a public protest and restored. The thatched roof was renewed in 1965, and it was advertised for sale in 1970. Despite considerable interest it was not sold. In 1975 it was destroyed by fire again and vandalised, after which the council again decided to demolish it. The Birkenhead History Society objected and were given thirty days to come up with a scheme to save it. This they did by forming a charitable trust with the local authority to develop the building as a field study centre for use by local schoolchildren. The building was restored using grants from the Manpower Services Commission, and it was leased to the trust for a rent of one pine cone per annum. It opened in May 1977.

Since 1986 it has become an Urban Farm under the auspices of the Wirral Urban Farm Association, which together with the Trust have developed additional buildings to house a collection of farm animals in the 4 acres surrounding the cottage.

THE MOST PROMINENT LANDMARK FOR MILES AROUND

Bidston Windmill

Access

To the north of Vyner Road North.

There has been a windmill on this site since at least 1596. The earlier mills were wooden peg mills, and evidence of one, in the form of a series of trenches and a circle of small holes, lies near the present structure. The current tower windmill was built in 1800 and was a replacement for the previous mill which had burnt down in 1791 after a gale had caused the arms to break loose and the resulting friction led to the fire. This mill has also been damaged by fire on a number of occasions, including 1832 and 1839, as well as suffering structural damage caused by the high winds which blow on this exposed ridge.

The mill last produced flour in 1875. It was restored by Robert Hudson of Boston in 1894 in commemoration of the opening of Bidston Hill to the public. Further restorations took place in 1927, in the 1970s, and in 1982 when the sails were replaced. It was damaged again in 1993. In recent years it has been open to the public on one Sunday a month, but now appears to be in need of further restoration and is closed.

Nearby, cut into the exposed rock, is a series of circular holes. These date from about 1763 and were used to hold the poles of the various signalling systems that were used to warn Liverpool ship owners of the imminent arrival of their ships in the days before radio and other means of communication. There are a great number of holes stretching all the way from the windmill to the lighthouse and the combined array was a distinctive feature of the hill. Some were provided by ship owners, and the rest were intended to warn of approaching warships. The system was based on the use of flags, but declined from 1827 when the Liverpool Dock Trustees established their telegraph system from Holyhead to Liverpool. All the visual systems ended in 1861 when a cable was laid that allowed the much more reliable electric telegraph to be introduced.

WHERE HIGH TIDES ANYWHERE IN THE WORLD COULD BE PREDICTED

Observatory, Bidston Hill

Access

Up the hill, due west of the junction between Vyner Park Road and Boundary Road.

The observatory was built by the Mersey Docks and Harbour Board in 1866 for astronomical and meteorological observations to assist shipping. The location at Bidston, away from the pollution of a rapidly developing Liverpool, was at the time considered more suitable for this work. The observatory had previously been located at Waterloo Dock in Liverpool from 1844.

In 1929 the observatory's work was merged with that of the Liverpool University Tidal Institute. Its work has evolved over the years and includes weather forecasting, tide predicting, measuring land movements and measuring the width of the Atlantic. Its most celebrated achievement was the invention and perfection of machinery that could accurately predict the high tides for anywhere in the world, and for any date, whether in the past or in the future. This machine, together with a telescope from the observatory's southern dome and an Astronomical Regulator Clock used in the observatory and built by William Bond of Boston in 1867, is on display in the Liverpool Museum.

Until 1969 the observatory was responsible for sending the electrical signal which set off the noon-day gun, which was a loud time signal fired from a cannon in Morpeth Dock in Birkenhead, and which was used by local workers as a signal that their lunch hour had come to an end. Since then a similar gun has been fired on special occasions from another location.

The observatory was extended in the 1970s when the John Proudman building was built to hold a new computer system, and became the Centre for Coastal and Marine Sciences – Proudman Oceanographic Laboratory. Closure of the observatory was mooted in 1994 and 2002, and finally took place in 2005, when it was relocated within the university area of Liverpool. The building is currently empty awaiting a new use.

To the north of the observatory stands Bidston Lighthouse. The first lighthouse was built here in 1771 to replace the one at Leasowe (see page 142) that had been destroyed in a storm. The current building was rebuilt in 1871/2, but was last used in 1913.

The wall to the west of the footpath that runs alongside the lighthouse is of great antiquity. It was originally built as the boundary wall when Bidston Hill was enclosed as a deer park in 1407, and is called 'Penny a Day Dyke' after the rate of pay for the men who built it.

BUILT AS A REPLICA OF A COTTAGE ON THE FOUNTAINS ABBEY ESTATE

Former Tweed House, Bidston Village

Access

On the south side of Bidston Village Road, close to the junction with Boundary Road. The building is private property.

This unassuming stone-built property, which blends in well with the surrounding older buildings of Bidston village, is remarkable in that it is an almost exact 'mirror-image' replica of a cottage on the Fountains Abbey estate in Yorkshire. The latter is close to the Fountains Hall entrance to the estate, and was built in about 1743 by the Messenger family. In recent years it was used by the National Trust as a shop and is currently two holiday cottages, known as Abbey Cottage and Abbey Stores Cottage.

The Bidston village property was built in late 1937 as a combined house and shop by local landowner Commander Clare George Vyner. The Vyners had owned substantial holdings in the area since the late seventeenth to early eighteenth century, when Robert Vyner, Lord Mayor of London, goldsmith and money lender, had acquired the estate through foreclosure on a loan. The link between the two properties comes from the Vyners who in the 1930s also owned the Fountains Abbey Estate. This they had inherited from the Aislabies who had acquired it in 1767, and who are noted for creating the impressive landscaping and water gardens of the adjoining Studley Royal estate.

The shop, located on what was then a main road to Hoylake, was built as an outlet for tweed probably produced on the Vyner estates in the Western Isles and woven in factories in Yorkshire. The first tenant was a Mrs Catherine Thompson, the widow of the former village policeman, who had impressed Commander Vyner with her enterprise in running a small store in a nearby cottage after the death of her husband. The property became known as the Tweed House.

The use of the shop to sell tweed was short lived and had ended by early 1939, by which time it was being used to sell sweets. For a time during the Second World War, the shop was not used, but afterwards functioned as the general village store until the late 1960s. A café operated in the gardens in the postwar years, catering for visitors to Bidston Hill.

Parts of the village had a neglected look in the later years of Vyner ownership, until the properties were sold off between the late 1960s and the early 1980s. The former Tweed House was extensively renovated in the early 1980s, and is now two separate private houses known as Fern Cottage and Tweed Cottage.

Opposite St Oswald's Church is Church Farm, a medieval building in which no two rooms are on the same level. There are no fewer than thirteen different floor levels in the house, and thirteen different flights of stairs. It was once thought to have been some sort of monastic building, but this is now considered unlikely. Church Farm was featured in the BBC television series *The House Detectives*.
See also nearby, on the eastern side of the Bidston Avenue/Tollemache Road junction, Birkenhead's oldest inhabited house, known as Toad Hole Farm Cottage. It is thought to have been erected in about 1530.

BIDSTON HILL'S MYSTERIOUS ROCK CARVINGS

Access

This is rather difficult to find, but is approximately west of Hillside Farm on Boundary Road (B5151).

Sun Goddess Carvings, Bidston Hill

The rock outcrops on Bidston Hill contain a number of mysterious carvings. This one, roughly 4½ft long, is of a sun goddess, with outstretched arms and the sun's rays at her feet. Her head points north-east in exactly the direction of the setting sun on Midsummer's Day. Various dates, from the second century onwards, have been suggested for this particular carving, but it is currently thought to be Norse Irish.

Another carving on Bidston Hill shows a Moon Goddess with a cat-like head and a moon at her feet. Others show human figures and horses cut into the vertical sandstone face on the western side of the ridge. These are thought to be more recent creations, dating from the eighteenth and nineteenth centuries.

IN COMMEMORATION OF 'MUDBOREE'

Memorial to World Boy Scout Jamboree, Arrowe Park

Access

Located within
the landscaping
at the front of
Arrowe Park
Hospital, on the
western side of
Arrowe Park
Road (A551).

The World Boy Scout Jamboree was held in Arrowe Park between 31 July and 13 August 1929. The jamboree was to have been held in Czechoslovakia, but the location was changed to celebrate the movement's twenty-first birthday, which had originated in nearby Birkenhead.

Over 50,000 boy scouts from all parts of the world attended, together with some 320,000 members of the public, and it was a success. Owing to heavy rain thick mud developed on the site, and the title Mudboree was born. Many who attended however, thought that the boys' good humour in facing this problem only increased the sense of lasting enjoyment that the event generated. Old copies of the special site newspaper, the *Daily Arrowe*, can still be seen in the local history libraries.

The small statue (seen below), by Edward Carter Preston, was unveiled in 1931 at the Five Ways Meet in Arrowe Park, by Lord Hampton, the movement's headquarters commissioner. The idea for a memorial to the event had been suggested in the local press a couple years earlier. The statue was removed for cleaning and restoration in 1981 and restored by Terry Price with funding from the scout movement. It was re-unveiled by the chief scout on its new site in June 1983.

'THE FIRST AND ONLY GOOD HOUSING ESTATE IN ENGLAND'

Port Sunlight

Access

The simplest access is via Bolton Road which leads off the roundabout at the southern end of the New Ferry bypass (A51).

Port Sunlight was the brainchild of William Hesketh Lever, later Lord Leverhulme, when he conceived the idea of a garden village to house the workers for his new factory producing Sunlight soap. He was a man of high ideals, wanting better surroundings for his workers than were common at the time. At Port Sunlight his ideals were to be fulfilled.

Initially, some 56 acres were bought in 1888 for the price of £200 per acre, 24 acres for the factory and the rest for the village. Work started on some cottages (on Bolton Road) and an entrance lodge in 1888–90 to a layout planned by Lever himself, although in time some thirty architects were to be involved in the project. The plans included good-quality housing and large areas of open space for recreation. Two large schools, a hospital, a swimming pool and gymnasium, library, museum, shops, village halls, social clubs, a public house (the Bridge Inn, originally a temperance hotel) and the imposing Christ Church were all built. By the time the scheme was finished in 1934 the village extended to 130 acres, had 850 houses and 72 flats, and housed a population of over 4,000.

A wide variety of architectural styles is evident in the housing and no two groups of houses are the same. There is much red brick and timberwork showing Tudor influences, but Queen Anne and Dutch styles are also evident. Building materials and the architectural detailing of doors, windows and chimney-stacks show a similar variety.

The central attraction of Port Sunlight is the Lady Lever Art Gallery, built in between 1914 and 1922 as a memorial to his wife, Elizabeth Ellen. It is an impressive building, containing a superb collection of national significance, all collected by Lever. On one side of the building is a memorial to Lever himself, but within such a village this seems superfluous.

After Lever's death in 1927 the factory and estate became part of the Unilever empire. Properties on the estate are no longer only occupied by Unilever employees, and began to be sold off to sitting tenants from 1980, although the ownership of front gardens was retained. The public facilities are now under the control of the Port Sunlight Village Trust. The standard of the estate remains very high, with good maintenance and effective estate management control. Satellite dishes, ill-sited caravans, vandalism, graffiti or stone effect cladding cannot be seen here; instead there are well-tended gardens, floral displays and evidence of some sense of community.

The Heritage Centre on Greendale Road has good displays on the development of the village.

'A RARE EXAMPLE OF A WAR MEMORIAL THAT IS GENUINELY MOVING AND AVOIDS SENTIMENTALITY'

War Memorial, Port Sunlight

Access

At the junction of The Causeway, Queen Mary's Drive and King George's Drive.

This war memorial, called 'Defence of the Home', is one of the most impressive in the country. Forming another focal point within the village on a roundabout, it was designed by William Goscombe John (who had designed the *Titanic* Engineers' Memorial in Liverpool).

Lever asked John to do the work in 1916. It was unveiled on 3 December 1921 by Sergeant E.G. Eames from Port Sunlight, who had lost his sight at the First Battle of the Somme in 1916, and by Private R.E. Cruikshank of the firm's London office, who had been awarded the Victoria Cross in 1918.

The memorial contains the names of all those from the company who lost their lives in the First World War, listed alphabetically. There is a separate list relating to the Second World War.

The memorial is constructed from granite and bronze. The central Runic cross is surrounded by a life-like group of eleven figures. Soldiers guard women and children and a wounded comrade whom a nurse is about to tend. A seated women cradles a group of infants and a frightened little girl stands, guarded by an equally frightened but defiant younger brother, and a boy scout stands with the soldiers, protected.

Against the parapet of the surrounding enclosure are large bas relief panels depicting anti-aircraft activities with a Vickers gun in action; men of the Navy on the bridge of an armed trawler with a commander and a seaman scanning the sea for submarines and the helmsman at his post; a body of infantry firing a Lewis Gun; and the Red Cross, with children offering wreaths and garlands. The fact that more children than adults are depicted emphasises the 'Defence of the Home' theme of the memorial, and its meaning and intent cannot be under-rated.

A Memorial to a Local Eccentric

The Puzzle Stones of Thomas Francis, Bebbington

Access

In the foyer of Bebbington Library, located in Bebbington Civic Centre, between Civic Way and Village Road (B5136). Accessible only during library opening hours.

Thomas Francis was a stonemason, whose eccentricity in the area was legendary. Born in 1763, he cut these stones, also called the Riddle Inscriptions, and installed them in the walls of his house, situated opposite the foot of Heath Road. One suggestion for their installation was that he intended to prevent local idlers from using the frontage of his property as a meeting area. By setting them riddles they could not understand, he intended to ridicule them and cause them to move on. There are a number of stones. One is inscribed with 'A rubbing stone for Asses', while three others contain mathematical puzzles. One, now unrecognisable, contained a slightly sarcastic elegy to one Catherine Grey, a pottery seller from Chester.

Francis died in 1850 and was buried in a grave he had dug for himself in St Andrew's churchyard. His house was demolished in 1965 when the stones were moved to Mayer Park. They were moved to their present location in 1997 to prevent further weathering of the sandstone slabs.

A RAILWAY WHICH TRANSPORTED THE STONE TO BUILD BIRKENHEAD

Storeton Tramway

The former quarries on Stourton Hill provided a fine source of sandstone from Roman times up to the 1950s. Many fine buildings in the centre of Birkenhead, including the Town Hall (see page 126), parts of the docks, together with buildings in Liverpool, Essex and Ireland, are known to have been constructed with the material.

The Storeton Tramway, originally called Sir Thomas Massey Stanley's Railway, after the local landowner and owner of the quarries, opened on 15 August 1838. It ran for a distance of 2½ miles, and was designed to transport stone to Bromborough Pool. The line, which cost £12,000, was laid as a standard gauge single-track with passing loops, and was horse-drawn. It was reputedly laid with fish-bellied track that had originally been used on the Liverpool and Manchester Railway, but which by 1838 was having to be replaced because of the increasing weight of steam locomotives in use. The track was laid on stone blocks rather than wooden sleepers, and as such had more in common with the mineral tramways that were in use prior to the Railway Age.

A connection between the tramway and the Birkenhead to Chester Railway was put in at a later date, but traffic started to decline in the late nineteenth century, as local roads improved. Development of the Lever factory close to Bromborough Pool caused further disruption, and the tramway was last used in 1905. Its rails were lifted in the decades that followed, and other buildings associated with the tramway were demolished. The quarries at the northern end of the line were filled with waste from the construction of the Queensway Road Tunnel between Liverpool and Birkenhead in the early 1930s.

Much of the former line has now been built over, but some stone blocks remain within the grounds of Wirral Grammar School, and this very short length of line has been replaced within the footpath that runs along the old trackway through Storeton Woods.

Fossil footprints of dinosaurs, known as chirotherium, were discovered in the quarry at various times between 1838 and 1916, and examples found can be seen in the Liverpool Museum and at Rock Ferry in the porch of Christ Church and the entrance to the Victoria Hall.

A CHURCH TOWER WITH FIVE CLOCK FACES

All Saints' Church, Thornton Hough

Access

Via Church
Road, which runs
between Raby
Road and
Thornton
Common Road
(B5136).

The attractive village of Thornton Hough was originally named Toristone until the mid-fourteenth century. It acquired its present name when the daughter of Roger de Thornton married Richard de Hough at the time.

In the 1860s Joseph Hirst, a retired woollen manufacturer from Willshaw, near Huddersfield, made his mark on the village. After building himself Thornton House, in 1867–8 he built All Saints' Church (at a cost of £7,000) in the Early English style, the vicarage and local school, followed by some shops and houses. On the eastern side of the square church tower are two clock faces, a smaller one above the main face. This was to allow Hirst, to see the time on the church clock from his bedroom in Thornton House, as the face of the main clock was obscured by the apex of the church roof. Hirst's death in 1870 ended this phase of the village's development.

William Hesketh Lever moved into nearby Thornton Manor in 1888, shortly after he established his soap factory at what was to become Port Sunlight. His effect on the village was to be more radical. He effectively rebuilt all the pre-Hirst village, replacing the inadequate housing with three- to five-bedroom houses. Using the same architects as he was using in nearby Port Sunlight, he re-arranged the village and extended it by some twenty additional houses, giving it the horseshoe shape in has today, grouped around the village green. He also rebuilt the village smithy, and provided a post office, village club and institute and a large non-denominational school, replacing the earlier one built by Hirst.

He also built St George's Congregational Church, completed in May 1907, in what has been described as a 'purest Norman style'.

To the north of Thornton Hough and Thornton Manor is a 6-mile network of long tree-lined avenues, mostly closed to traffic, created by Lord Leverhulme in the early years of the twentieth century, as part of his typical 'estate improvement' activities. The longest of these, Lever Causeway, is open to traffic north of the village of Stourton, and connects with Mount Road (B5151).

WIRRAL'S OTHER PLANNED VILLAGE

Price's Village, Bromborough Pool

Access

Via Pool Lane,
off the eastern
side of New
Chester Road
(A41).

This village pre-dates its near neighbour, Port Sunlight, and dates from 1853 when James and George Wilson, directors of Price's Patent Candle Company, were seeking a site close to Liverpool. The firm had been established by the family in Battersea in 1830, but the cost and time of transferring the West African palm oil from the main port of entry at Liverpool, to London were considered excessive, and a booming demand for candles meant that a second factory site was required.

The site they found at Bromborough Pool enabled production to increase significantly. The Wilsons were benevolent employers and the firm introduced a profit-sharing scheme for employees in 1869 and a contributory pension scheme in 1893. They also built a model village for their workers, occasionally referred to as 'our colony on the Mersey'. It is one of the earliest such developments.

Thirty-two houses on York Street were the first to be built, catering for key workers brought from Battersea. All the houses were provided with internal toilets, a parlour, kitchen, scullery, three bedrooms and gardens. Phase two followed between 1872 and 1878 with houses on Manor Place, and further houses followed in the 1890s to make a total of 142 by 1901, housing some 728 people.

The overall design was by Julian Hill, who also designed the factory and the village hall. A chapel had been finished in 1890 and a new school in 1898. The village hall, dating from 1858, was also used at various times as a chapel, school, village shop and isolation hospital. Central to the whole scheme was the cricket ground, provided not only for recreational purposes, but also to foster team spirit and camaraderie.

In 1919 Prices were taken over by their rivals, Lever Brothers, and candle production at Bromborough ceased in 1936, with the works continuing with fatty acid production. It is today part of the Uniqema group. Only a small brick building with a clock tower remains of the original factory.

The village today, now managed by Merseyside Improved Homes, remains popular, although some of the communal facilities look a little unkempt. An exception to this is the former village hall, now the Giles Shirley Hall, which is run by the Wirral Autistic Society.

ONE OF THE OLDEST BUILDINGS ON WIRRAL

Spann's Tenement, Bromborough

Access

On the south side of Mark Rake, close to its junction with Chester Road (A41).

This fine example of a seventeenth-century merchant's house, sometimes called Stanhope House, was built in 1693 on the site of an earlier house dating from Tudor times. A nameplate over the doorway is decorated with Tudor roses and contains the initials 'JSE', after Joseph and Elizabeth Spann.

After many years it passed into the ownership of the Whitelaw family. By the late eighteenth century it was owned by a Mr Ellis, who owned the Bromborough Mills. In the early 1930s it was bought by Mr A.H. Boulton, a local builder, who wanted to demolish it. After being refused permission, he gave it to Bromborough Council in 1937 in memory of his parents. In 1939 Bromborough Council opened it as a branch library and renovated it. Unfortunately this 'restoration' involved the removal of original oak panelling.

It was threatened with demolition again in 1964, but was saved after a local outcry and intervention by the Bromborough Society, which persuaded the owner of Gawsworth Hall in Cheshire, Mr Richards, to undertake its restoration, after taking a long lease at a peppercorn rent in 1966. During this work the former panelling in the Drawing Room was restored using panels from Chillingham Castle in Northumberland. It is now occupied by a firm of accountants.

Evidence of Early Christianity in Bromborough

Viking Age Cross, Bromborough

Access

In the churchyard of St Barnabas's Church, on Church Lane, to the right of the church porch.

This sandstone cross, thought to be either Saxon or Viking in origin, dates from about AD 900. It is a wheel-headed cross. At the centre of the cross, on both sides is a bird, which represents the Holy Spirit.

The cross is thought by some to be a 'preaching cross' and the product of the workshop that existed at St John's Church in Chester. Its remnants were found, along with those of other Saxon objects, when the previous Bromborough church, built in 1829, was being demolished in the 1860s. Some of these remnants were placed in the garden of the rectory, while those of the cross were placed on the window sills of the south porch of the church. The cross was re-erected on this site by the Bromborough Society in 1958 to mark the Society's Silver Jubilee.

Nearby, on The Rake in the centre of the road, is Bromborough Cross, which marks the site of the borough's weekly market held from 1278 under a charter granted to the monks of St Werburgh's Abbey in Chester by Edward I. This cross has components of three ages. The seven sandstone steps at the bottom date from the thirteenth century. The column and neo-Gothic structure date from 1874, while the top cross dates from the 1970s when the Bromborough Society replaced thè original which had been stolen in the 1960s.

A TREE THOUGHT TO BE OVER 1,000 YEARS OLD

Eastham Old Yew

Access

Within the churchyard of St Mary's Church, at the junction of Eastham Village Road and Stanley Lane.

The exact age of this tree is not known. Some put it as old as 1,500 years. In 1898 members of the Royal Archaeological Society expressed the view that it may have been planted against the east end of a timber-framed wattle and daub chapel erected some time before 1066. In 1152, when the Manor of Eastham came under the control of the abbot and monks of St Werburgh's in Chester, the villagers asked the new owners 'to have a care of the olde yew'.

In the days when bows and arrows were made of yew, every parish was compelled by law to have at least one yew tree growing in its churchyard. The tree has shown signs of decay for many years. In the 1980s Alan Brack, author of *The Wirral*, attempted unsuccessfully to get the tree listed in the *Guinness Book of Records* as the oldest tree in Britain.

The adjacent St Mary's Church has a breech spire and is said to be one of only two such spires in Wirral. It dips over the parapet of the tower, and appears to be unsupported.

ONCE KNOWN AS THE 'RICHMOND OF THE MERSEY'

Eastham Ferry and Country Park

Eastham was once an important point for those making journeys between Liverpool and Chester in the days before the railways and better road communications. It was the place where passengers travelling by ferry were obliged to change to road transport for the final stage of the trip to Chester.

The monks of Chester Abbey first began the ferry service from Eastham to Liverpool. It was mentioned in the Domesday Book and by 1509 was known as 'Job's Ferry', and later as 'Carlett's Ferry'. In 1815 the first steam vessel was put into use, and the following year Samuel Smith introduced the paddle steamer *Princess Charlotte* which cut the time from Chester to Liverpool from 4 to 2¼ hours.

The importance of the ferry route started to decline in 1833 when Thomas Brassey's New Chester Road was completed allowing a quicker route via Birkenhead. In 1840 the Chester to Birkenhead railway was built.

In 1846 the Eastham Ferry Hotel was built by Sir William Massey Stanley. The following year the estate, ferry and hotel passed to Richard Naylor, a Liverpool merchant. He decided to develop Eastham as a pleasure garden to revive the

fortunes of the ferry. A fairground, band concerts, circus acts, zoo, flower gardens, hobby horses, water chute and a famous 'loop-the-loop' ride were all introduced. An open-air stage, ballroom, boating lake and tea rooms all operated. A Jubilee arch was built at the entrance to the gardens; it is reputed to have been re-erected here after being taken down from another site in Liverpool. The zoological collection comprised lions, tigers, bears, antelopes, seals, a monkey house and an aviary. George Mottershead, who founded Chester Zoo in the 1930s, is reputed to have witnessed cruelty to an elephant here, which led to his resolution to run his new institution with much more emphasis on animal welfare. Blondin (Jean Francis Gravelier), the famous Niagara Falls tightrope walker, performed at Eastham on more than one occasion.

In 1874 a new iron pier was built. By this time Eastham was known as the 'Richmond of the Mersey' (after the town by the Thames), attracting thousands of visitors from Liverpool. In the 1890s the ferries bore the names *Ruby*, *Sapphire* and *Pearl*.

The pier had to be rebuilt in 1911 but owing to declining popularity of the gardens, the ferry ceased in 1929. The Jubilee arch and the pier were both demolished in the early 1930s and the ballroom burnt down in the 1950s.

Today Eastham is the venue for a popular Country Park. The hotel remains, along with the bear pit, a small stub remaining of the pier and this small sandstone building, originally the ferry ticket office. An interesting visitor centre gives more details of the place's history.

INDEX

Aintree Racecourse 82
Albert Dock 14, 24
Alexandra Park 105
Allerton Oak 56
Alphabet Stone, Prescot 77
All Saints' Church, Childwall 53
All Saints' Church, Thornton
    Hough 167
Alsop, Will 12
Ancient Chapel of Toxteth 67
Anderton Shearer Mining
    Monument 107
Andre, Edouard 61
Anfield Stadium 40, 41
Archway, Newton le Willows 116
Arrowe Park 161
Ashton, the Revd Ellis 75
Atlantic Conveyor 15
Atomic Kitten 21

Baden Powell, Lord 26, 161
Barnston Towers 153
Barberi, Blessed Dominic 114–15
beacons 39, 112
Beatles, The 14, 21, 59–60, 65
Beecham Clock Tower 110
'Bibby Land' 55
Bibby, John 55
Bidston Court 70
Bidston Hill signalling systems 155
Bidston Lighthouse 157
Bidston Observatory 156–7
Bidston Windmill 155
Billinge Beacon 112
Birkenhead Park 127
Birkenhead Town Hall 126
Birkenhead Tramway 124
Black Chair, Eisteddfod of the 128
Blackler, Philip 82
'Blondin' 173
'Bloody Acre' 53
Blundell family 85–8, 90–1, 115
Boode, Margaret 141
Boot Inn, Wallasey 132

Botanical Gardens 47, 95, 101
Boulder Stone, Crosby 83
Boy Scout Jamboree 161
Bretherton, Bartholomew 122
Brick Wall Inn, Tarbock 174
Brimstage Hall and Tower 152
Bromborough Society, The 169–70
Bronington, HMS 129
Brookside set 43, 49
Brunel, Isambard Kingdom 40
'Burgy Banks' 104
Bushell, Ma 39
Butler, Edward 15

Calderstones Park 47, 54
canals 104
Capital of Culture award 7, 29
Carletts Ferry 172
Carnarvon Castle pub 20
'Cast Iron Shore' 69
Castle, Roy 28
cathedrals
    Anglican 11, 30
    Catholic 36
Cavern Club 21
cemeteries 28, 31–3, 171
Central Park, New York 127
Charles Dawson Brown Museum,
    West Kirby 147
Chavasse Park 29, 70
Childwall Abbey 53
Chieso, Taro 29
Chinese Arch 28
churches and chapels 15, 28–30, 33
    53, 67, 88–90, 109, 113–15,
    122, 133, 147, 67, 171
Church Farm, Bidston 159
Church of the Three Saints 114–15
Churchtown 95, 101–2
Civil War 10, 39
Clarke, Sir Kenneth 105
Cleaver, Mrs Babcock 56
Cochrane & Company 24
Cockerell, C.R. 22

Corlett, Harry 63
Cotton Exchange 17
Cronton Cross 75
crosses 75, 79, 118, 170
Cuckoo Clock, Woolton Woods 63
Cunard Building 11–12

Dagnall, Tom 106
Derby House 19
'Dickie Lewis' 23
'Dockers Umbrella' 68
Dock Office 14
Downward, Mr 18

Eastham Ferry and Country Park
    172
Eastham Old Yew 171
Eisteddfod commemoration
    stone, Birkenhead Park 128
'Eleanor Rigby' 21
Elmes, Harvey Lonsdale 22
Emslie Morgan 140
Epstein, Brian 21
Epstein, Jacob 23
Eros Fountain, Sefton Park 61
Evans, Councillor David 128
Evans, Ellis Humphrey, *see* Hedd
    Wynn
Everton Beacon 39
Everton Football Club 39
Exchange Flags 18

Falkner Square 34
ferries 12, 37, 130, 138, 172
Five Lamps War Memorial,
    Crosby 84
Fleishman, Arthur 107
Forthlin Road 59
Fort Perch, New Brighton 136–7
Foster, John (senior and junior)
    27–8, 31, 33
fountains 105
Frampton, George 108
Francis, Thomas 165

French, Percy 93
Friends Meeting House, St Helens 109
Fry, Maxwell 105

'Games', Wallasey 130
Gateacre Gazebo 62
Gerard, Thomas 111
'Giant Grasshopper' 125
Gibberd, Sir Frederick 36
Gladstone, William Ewart 27
Godstone, Formby 93
Goscombe John, Sir William 13, 164
Graham, Gillespie 126–7
Grand National 62, 82, 143
Great Eastern 40
Greek Orthodox Church 67
Guide Dog statue, New Brighton 138
Gustav Adolph Church 29

'Ham and Eggs Parade', New Brighton 138
Hardwick, Philip 14
Harkirk Chapel, Little Crosby 86
Harris, Thomas 15
Harthill 55
Hartley, Jesse 55, 121
Hartley Pillar 55
Hartley Village 44
Hedd Wynn 128
Herculaneum Dock 68
Herdman, W.A. 54
Highton, Luke 94
Hilbre Island 148–9
Hillsborough Memorial 41
Hirst, Joseph 167
Historic Warships, Birkenhead 129
Hoare, Elizabeth 30
'Hole in the Wall Church' 113
Hornblower, Lewis 61, 127
Hornby, Frank 89
Hoylake Upper Light 144
Huskisson, William 32, 120
Huyton Cross 75

Ireland, Lawrence 58, 90

'Jane Harrison' 84
Jet of Iada 56
Job's Ferry 172
Jones, Bronwen and Gwladys 113

Kavanagh, Peter 35
Kelly, Theo 39
Kirkby Cross 79
Knotty Ash 18
Knowsley Village 78
Krowlow, Hugh 110

Lakeside Inn 100
Laird family 126
Landings Roundabout, St Helens 106
Lady Lever Art Gallery 163
'Law Oak' 56
Lea, Richard 154
Leasowe Castle 141
Leasowe Lighthouse 142
Lennon, John 21, 26, 60
letter boxes 24
Lever Causeway 167
Leverhulme Estates 91
Lever, William Hesketh 162–4, 167
Lewis's 23, 40
Liberty Park, West Kirby 146
lifeboat station (former), Hilbre 149
Lion's Gate Lodge, Ince Blundell 87
Liscard Battery 135
Liscard Magazines 135
Liver Birds 10, 12
Liverpool Airport 71–2
Liverpool and Manchester Railway 121
Liverpool Castle 16
Liverpool Garden Festival 29, 69
Liverpool Garden Suburb Tenants Ltd 52
Liverpool Marriott South Hotel 72
Liverpool Overhead Railway 68
'Liverpool Resurgent' statue 23
lock-ups 23, 48
Lord Street, Southport 95–7
Lowe House, St Helens 106
Lusitania Propeller 14
Lutyens, Sir Edwin 36
Lydiate Hall 90–1

McCain, 'Ginger'
McCartney, Paul 59
McDona, the Revd Cuming 145
Mackenzie & Moncur 61
McKenzie, W. 27
Maghull Chapel 89
Mariners' Column, West Kirby 146

Market House, Newton le Willows 116
markets 17, 116
Marsden, Gerry 21, 41
Marshside Fog Bell 102
Mason, 'Titch' 143
Matear & Simeon 17
Mathew Street 21
Mendips 60
Mersey Docks Board 11
'Mersey Funnel', see cathedral, Catholic
Merseyside Development Corporation 69–70
Merseyside Maritime Museum 14
'Milly Stone', Earlestown 118
Molyneaux, Richard 74
Monks' Well 50
Moreton Cross 143
Moreton-Rhyl hovercraft service 142
'Mother Redcap' 131
'Mudboree' 161

National Trust 59–60, 158
Nelson memorials 18
New Double Locks, St Helens 104
Noble, Sir Percy 19

Oddfellows 74
Old Court House, West Derby 42
Olmstead, F.L. 127
Ono, Yoko 60
Onyx, HMS 129
Organs 22, 30, 150
Owen, Wilfred 128

'Paddy's Wigwam', see cathedral, Catholic
Palm House, Sefton Park 61
Parks 15, 18, 47, 50, 54–6, 61, 63–4, 69–70, 83, 101, 127–8, 146, 161, 172
Parkside 120
Paxton, Joseph 127
'Penny a Day Dyke' 157
Penny Lane 60
Peter Kavanagh 35
Peter Pan, Sefton Park 61
Philharmonic Dining Rooms 26
Philharmonic Hall 25
Picton, James 48–9, 51
Pigeon House, Kirkby 80
Pilkington Head Office site 105

Pipe and Gannex pub, Knowsley 78
'Plymouth', HMS 129
Pooley, Sarah 49
Port Sunlight 162–4
Post & Echo War Memorial,
    Exchange Flags 18
Potters Barn, Waterloo 83
Prescot Folly 76
Price's Village, Bromborough 168
Prince Rupert 39
Princes Road Synagogue 67
Prout, Elizabeth 114
public houses 20, 26, 35, 74, 92,
    100, 132, 143
Pugin, A.W. and E.W. 36
Puzzle Stones 165

Queen Victoria 16, 108

Rainhill Skew Bridge 121
Randall & Sons 116
Rawlinson, Robert 22
Redcap, Mother 131
Redmond, Phil 43
Red Nose and Yellow Noses
    Rocks, New Brighton 139
Red Rum 82, 98
Rensburg, Henry 25
'Richmond of the Mersey' 172
'River Mersey', statue of the 17
Robert Cain & Sons 26
Robin Hood's Stone 57
Roby Cross 75
Roscoe, William 47
Roosevelt, Eleanor 38
Round House, Birkdale 94
Rowse, Herbert 25
Royal Liver Building 10–12
Royden Park 70
Roza, Lita 21

sailors' church 10, 15
St Aidan's Church, Billinge 112
St Andrew's Church, Maghull 89
St Bartholomew's Church,
    Rainhill 122
St Catherine's Chapel, Lydiate 90
St Chad's Cross, Kirkby 79
St George's Church, Thornton
    Hough 167
St George's Hall 22–3
St Helen's Church, Sefton 86, 88
St Helens Mining Monument 106
St Helens and Sankey Canal 104

St Hilary's Church, Wallasey 133
St James's Park 31–3
St Mary's Church, Eastham 171
St Mary's RC Church, St Helens 106
Salisbury Dock 37
Salisbury, Lord 42, 50
Salisbury Stone 50
Sanctuary Stone 16
Sandy Knowe, Wavertree 51
Scotch Piper pub, Lydiate 92
Scott, Sir Giles Gilbert 30
Scott, Sir Walter 51
Sefton Park 61
'Sephton Corporation' 88
Shankly Gates 41
Shaw, George 109
Shaw, Norman 12
Shore Road Pumping Station 125
Sgt Pepper's Bistro 60
Smith, John 115
Soarer Cottages, Gateacre 62
Solar Campus 140
Southport 93–100
Spann's Tenement, Bromborough
    169
Speakers' Corner, Wallasey 130
Spencer, Ignatius 114
Springfield Park 18
Stanlawe Grange 58
Stanley Dock 38
Stevenson, George and Robert 121
Stirling, Edwin 55
stocks 75, 93, 117
Stone Street, Prescot 76
Storeton Quarries 166
Strawberry Fields 60
Steele, Tommy 21
Sun Goddess Carving, Bidston
    Hill 160
Superlamb Banana 29
Sutton Stone, Southport 95

Tam O' Shanter Urban Farm,
    Bidston 154
telegraph station (former), Hilbre 148
Tell's Tower 145
'Three Graces' 11
Thomas, Aubrey 10
Thomas Francis Puzzle Stones 165
Thompson, Henry Yates 61
Thornley, Arthur 11
Thornton Hough 167
Thor's Stone, Thurstaston 151
Thurstaston Country Park 149

Titanic Band Memorial 25
Titanic Engineers Memorial 13
Toad Hall Farm Cottage 159
Town Halls 77, 108, 126, 130
Train, George Francis 124
trams 84, 124
Tweed House (former), Bidston 158

U-534, German submarine 129
Unsworth Chapel 89

Vestey Tower 30
Vicarage Place, Prescot 77
Victoria Square, St Helens 108
Victoria Tower 37
Viking Age Cross, Bromborough
    170
Vulcan Village 119
Vyner family 158

Wallasey Grammar School 134
Wallasey Town Hall 130
Wall of Fame 21
War Memorial, Port Sunlight 164
Wavertree Botanical Gardens 47
Wavertree Garden Suburb 52
Wavertree Lake 50
Wavertree lock-up 48
Wayfarer's Arcade, Southport 98
Weeping Stone, Kirkby 79
Wellington Column 22
Welsh Chapel, Sutton Oaks 113
Western Approaches Museum 19
Westmacott, Richard 18
White Star Line 12
Williamson, Joseph 45–6
Williamson Square 29
Williamson Tunnels 45–6
Willink & Thicknesse 12
Wilson, Harold 78, 134
Wilson Memorial Fountain 62
Windleshaw Chantry 111
windmills 85, 155
Wirral Autistic Society 168
Wirral Museum 126
Woodside Ferry Terminal 124, 126
Woolton Cinema 65
Woolton Old School 66
Woolton Woods 63
Wyatt, Mathew Coles 18

Yarrow, Lady Annette 98
Ye Hole in ye Wall pub 20
'You'll Never Walk Alone' 41